ALICE FOOTE MACDOUGALL

THE AUTOBIOGRAPHY OF
A BUSINESS WOMAN

WITH ILLUSTRATIONS

BOSTON
LITTLE, BROWN, AND COMPANY
1928

Published February, 1928

THE ATLANTIC MONTHLY PRESS PUBLICATIONS

ARE PUBLISHED BY

LITTLE, BROWN, AND COMPANY

IN ASSOCIATION WITH

THE ATLANTIC MONTHLY COMPANY

PRINTED IN THE UNITED STATES OF AMERICA

ALICE FOOTE MACDOUGALL

TO WOMEN — WHOM I LOVE AND
WOULD HELP — I DEDICATE MY BOOK

My dear Alice:

I have just learned that you are putting on record your "Twenty Years Hard Labor", which enabled you so happily to bring up and educate your children and provide amply for your own and their future comfort. I feel proud to have been of some little help in this and extend to you my heartiest congratulations on your exceptional success.

Every one is thrilled by acts of heroism or achievements against great odds, and I am no exception to the rule. But your life work, with which I have been familiar, challenges my admiration to the utmost. Yours was the heroism of a daily struggle in cold blood to make a place for yourself in the business world when that world was none too hospitable to the woman worker. To this discouraging task your valiant soul brought a courage and tenacity that accomplished so much.

Your book will be an encouragement and help to others similarly situated in showing how intelligent persevering industry reaps its reward. I rejoice in your success.

Affectionately,
Geo. F. Baker

Mrs. Alice Foote MacDougall

FACSIMILE LETTER FROM MR. GEORGE F. BAKER TO MRS. MACDOUGALL

ACKNOWLEDGMENT

In gratitude and appreciation, I hereby tender my thanks to Mr. M. A. DeWolfe Howe, Miss Teresa S. Fitzpatrick, and Mrs. Harry A. Stewart. Without their good advice this book, I fear, would have little worth.

FOREWORD

It is futile to ask women not to go into business, as futile almost as to insist that water shall not run downhill. One cannot stop world movements; and the efforts of women toward emancipation — the natural result of the deadly monotony of their task on the one hand, a jealousy of man's freedom, and a total ignorance of man's struggle as well as of the glory of their own special opportunity — all lead to the condition we are facing to-day.

From totally other causes and from an entirely opposite point of view, life forced me into business. At forty years of age I was left with thirty-eight dollars in the bank as capital, and three babies at home as assets. I had no business training or experience of any kind, but I determined to find within myself the ability to support my children. The following pages tell the story of the twenty years' hard labor I put in to accomplish my purpose.

If in any way I can indicate the pain of the struggle, if I can succeed in making women appreciate that there are two sides to the question, one not altogether rosy, and that, although they will undoubtedly win, they will be forced to pay a high price, then I shall have accomplished my purpose.

ALICE FOOTE MacDOUGALL

CONTENTS

ILLUSTRATIONS

ALICE FOOTE MACDOUGALL

THE AUTOBIOGRAPHY OF
A BUSINESS WOMAN

I

CHILDHOOD

I was born in the home of my mother's grand-father, Stephen Allen, at Number 1 North Washington Square, New York, on the second day of March, 1867. He was known as "Honest Stephen Allen," and was mayor of the city of New York from 1821 to 1824. To him and to my father's father, Homer Foote, and to my own beloved father, Emerson Foote, I owe whatever I have of business ability.

The first great affection of my life was born out of the tender care my Quaker grandmother, Catherine Maria Leggett Allen, gave me during my first five years, while my frail mother struggled back to health after my birth. She all but gave her life that I might have life.

To-day, as I drive past my birthplace, a vision of my father rises to my mind. On the night I was born he wandered, despairing, lonely, through the Square, praying to God that the young wife whom he adored might live. In later years, I too wandered, sometimes in the midst of seething lower Broadway, when the noon hour carried hundreds of light-hearted men and women to laugh and loiter on the busy thoroughfare, sometimes under the cold beautiful skies of a wintry night, alone in that irrevocable aloneness of sorrow, and prayed as did my father, to the same God, for my own life, for life to live bravely, forcefully, for my little children.

What is the root of our affection? Is it possible that even a tiny newborn infant can sense this all-pervading guardian love, and cling to it throughout life? I do not know. But to my dainty, sweet, Quaker grandmother I still cling. She was the only daughter in a family of eleven children, exquisitely beautiful, petulant, gay, and lovable. She was born to be adored, and she was, not only by her father, mother, and the ten big brothers, but by her husband, William Mortimer Allen, who used laughingly to call her "the Dragon." Yet in a long, grave illness which came upon him, with patient devotion did the Dragon tend him.

This grandmother loved me with imagination. She was patient when I was impatient, tolerant in an amused kind of way of my many vagaries, and always filled with tenderness and understanding for my woes, whether I wept over the cracked head of Minnie, my beloved doll, or the passing of faith in some friend I adored. There were plenty of times when I was everything a child should not be, spoiled, erratic, too imaginative.

How delightful those first five years were, and

what funny memories creep out of that past! True to my later anti-suffrage, anti-feminist proclivities, I was then very much of a little girl-mother, and wonderful and varied was the life I led with my many doll children. Minnie, named for my mother, was a substantial china-headed American lady of wobbly cotton body and fixed and permanent smile. My mother-heart opened wide its portals of love to her and never did later and smarter-looking children cause me to forget her entirely. Of course, when Papa, returning from Paris, brought Lillie with him, her modish clothes, beautiful blonde hair, real kid body, and delicate face, cast Minnie quite into the shade. I did Lillie the credit to think she wanted to express her æstheticism, and so I tried to teach her to play the piano. But she fell off the stool. I can remember how I howled as her lovely face broke in two. For long she rested quietly on an attic shelf, where I tenderly nursed her. But moths invaded her golden tresses, and Mamma said, "Toots, why on earth do you want to keep that broken toy?" Cruel, good-housekeeping Mamma — only a mothy, broken toy to her; to me, a crippled child in very fact.

When I was about five, Mamma and I accompanied Papa on one of his many business trips to Europe. Remembrances of that trip are still vivid. A breaded chop on board the City of Brussels made me weep tears of homesickness for Jane, our cook at home. Arrived in London, all my affection was given to a little black-and-tan terrier, Lufra by name, and my loyalty to that horrid little brute kept two perfectly good maids and one small pernickety child from seeing the glories of Westminster Abbey. A mild, gentlemanly verger assured us that dogs were not allowed. Beseeching looks on the faces of the maids were of no avail. Small, bad, imperious Me said, "Where I go, goes my dog." So I dominated, and missed the joy of that inspiring relic. As a punishment, perhaps, I contracted whooping cough, and we hurried to Brighton till it should pass — punishment mitigated by many delights on the resplendent beach and on the backs of the patient donkeys whose business it was to carry small travelers.

And it was at this early age that Paris, gay, beautiful, and alluring, captivated my awakening senses, and during all the years to come my memory was filled with dreams of its charm.

Returning with us on the City of Brussels was Livingstone, the great African explorer. He had brought with him a little African boy, Calulah. We used to play together on the deck, and I can remember a feeling of pity that was always present in my heart during our games as the big ship ploughed her way homeward. We talked to each other in a combination of sound and sign, but always I was wondering how this black-skinned little boy really felt, so far away from his mamma

and papa, and my small heart ached for him and
made me a trifle less selfish and exacting in our
games together. What potential sorrows lay before
him! Many times since I have thought of him
and wondered how fate had treated him.

In the early days of my childhood, our home on
Eleventh Street, New York, was quite an ordinary
affair, stereotyped and conventional, and the days
were prim with their well-regulated routine. But
all this passed me by. I lived in Fairyland and in
constant communion with all kinds of wonderful
beings, performing countless amazing deeds which
inevitably made of me a heroine. Occasional in-
terludes, in the form of governesses and parents,
removed me from this Land of Sheer Delight, just
as in later years God led me out of the Land of
Romance to place me in the path of duty. But
in my early days every morning brought the hope
of a new adventure and my imagination made
the dream come true. My real life was lived
with my doll children in the Land of Let's Pretend;
and as I played, mother care, mother responsibility, entered persuasively into my soul, and
made there a safe abiding place against the
advent of my own dear babies.

All my play and toys bore a certain relation to
my expected duties as a woman. Froebel was
gently Froebel-ing in the good old German way, but
his theories, like Charity, had so far remained
at home.

In later years the imagination that propelled my child mind played a vital part in bringing about my success. As I used to imagine conditions and opportunities for my dolls, my dogs, and my cats, so in later years my customers intrigued me to further imaginings. When I was five, Minnie, my doll, needed this or that for her soul or her digestive salvation. Later, when I was forty-five, Mrs. Smith quite unconsciously secured the ministrations of my imagination and became a G..C. (grateful customer) in consequence. Wiles and smiles that I used to subdue the evil spirits and bad fairies of my infant days worked their spells no less on importunate creditors in days to come.

Though wonderful and varied was the life I led with my doll children, "keeping store" interested me greatly, too. I took care of doll babies and kept store at one and the same time. It was a prophecy of what I was to do later in grim earnest.

A mocking bird was the means — or could have been the means — of indicating to my parents my particular calling. Papa loved flowers and dogs, horses and birds, and one of his acquisitions was a mocking bird. To make the bird comfortable and happy a large, a very large, cage was made, for Papa had an expansive nature. He was big in heart, big in mind and in body, and to him all things needed bigness. So the cage arrived, and Dick sang out a sweet content. But to Mamma, the practical, it presented an appalling problem.

Where should it stand, this mammoth cage? A table had to be especially built for it, and in the table was a row of divided drawers to hold the many necessities of an accomplished seamstress — spools of cotton, fine and coarse; needles; bits of lace and muslin for mending. Here, incidentally and all unwittingly, began the Alice Foote Mac-Dougall Coffee Houses; for day after day I played store and bought and sold to imaginary customers the dry goods of the mocking bird's table drawers.

But the greatest delights of all were the afternoon drives with Papa. He fancied trotting horses and in weather fair or foul we would sally forth. A long, slow progress up Fifth Avenue, where the stone pavement was bad for the horses' feet; a gentle swiftness through the Park, which was a little difficult, for the police — we did not say "cops" then — would not allow speeding, and by that time the mares resented the restraint; and then, with a tiny click, the faintest sound on my father's lips, and a loosening of the reins, the horses settled into their gait, trotting faster and faster.

It is cold, perhaps rainy, and clods of turf from unpaved avenues fly back into our faces, or perhaps snow is falling and we see our competitors through it. Always in our tingling ears is the pounding of the excited horses' feet, that curious snort of delight and excitement as a swifter horse passes us, or we, darting off into space, out-distance him.

Men were temperate in those days, but a "nip" of brandy or some other liquor was deemed an essential after a long day on Wall Street or an afternoon trotting on St. Nicholas Avenue. Papa took great pride in his wine cellar. He was accustomed to having wine at dinner always, not so much for himself as for the many English and French gentlemen who were his constant dinner guests. After our drive, Commodore Vanderbilt, Frank Work, Charles Lanier, Mr. Harbeck, or some other gentlemen would return with Papa to our home on Eleventh Street. Then Papa would set out his choicest wines for their delectation — brandy fifty years old, filling the room the moment it was uncorked with a delicious, indescribable aroma, whiskey, sherry, port, all choice and very old. Conversation sparkled and the open fire glowed, but not more warmly than did my father as he thus entertained his friends.

There was a transportation problem in the city even then, but it was a different sort from to-day's. Huge, lumbering, uncouth, uncomfortable busses bumped and banged over the crude pavements of New York in those days, the seventies, and my first approach in one of them to the business district of New York and my later business haunts was a journey of wild alarums and excitements when I was about five.

Grandpa Stephen used to say, "I don't want any poor grandchildren," and to guard against this he had purchased largely in what is now the lower part of the city. Consequently Wall and Front Streets were words familiar to my childish ears. On an eventful morning in early December in 1872, I boarded the bus at Eleventh Street to make my first journey to Wall Street to purchase Christmas gifts for our many relatives from an importer of East Indian and Chinese goods, a tenant of one of Grandpa Stephen's stores.

What wild imaginings, what "blank misgivings of a creature moving about in worlds not realized" were mine, as that old bus lumbered and bumped the long, long journey southward. It was so bitterly cold that my lamb's-wool coat and turban did little good. But in spite of cold and discomfort, no more thrilling event ever happened to explorer than to me on my first journey to Wall Street. Hobgoblins and gnomes inhabited the straw covering of the floor and peeped with malicious eyes from corners or jeered in fiendish glee at my discomfort. And as the driver returned Grandma's change in a small brown envelope through a mysterious hole in the roof, I did n't doubt but that some good fairy would hop out to put an end to their malicious intentions.

What wonder, then, that when the bus finally let us down, it was at the door of the very store where later my husband had his office, and where, following him, I entered the ranks. Chance? I don't think so; the fairies did it — the good, beneficent fairies who all along have helped me until finally the gnomes have been put to rout.

To-day that lower part of the city is still filled with romance for me. Not alone do the pungent odors of coffee and myrrh and frankincense fill the air after their long journeys from the Indies and South America, but if you have eyes to see and ears to hear, gay ladies and gentlemen of Holland walk happily up and down. It is hard to understand their somewhat uncouth language, but there they are, in high-heeled shoes, full skirts, or knickerbockers, wigs, and cocked hats. Even dear old George will appear once in a while if only to go to Fraunces' Tavern to bid his officers farewell.

What a comfort it was in the drear days of 1907–1908, when I first entered business, to walk on Maiden Lane surrounded by the gay, enchanting maidens of those early days and forget the terrible present !

Crossing Wall Street, at what is called the lower end, is Front Street. Years ago it fronted the East River and was a place of gayety and gardens, but as the city grew and space became precious, the city was built out into the river, and at present South Street and not Front Street comes to the water's edge. Here centre the shipping interests that carry on trade in fruit, in spices, and in coffee, and here loiter idly at their quays the splendid ships of our South American trade. Naturally, then, Front Street devotes its entire attention to the coffee and tea business.

A word about my forbears before I pass these first five years of my life. For because of my intangible inheritances from them, in traditions, in ideals, in attitudes of heart and mind, I owe them a debt of gratitude quite too vast for words to express.

My great-grandfather, Stephen Allen, in whose house I was born, was drowned before my birth, when the Henry Clay burned and sank in 1852 in the Hudson. New York owes him its first steps taken in sanitation to rid the city of yellow fever, and he was first to propose the Croton Aqueduct in order to ensure the city an adequate and wholesome supply of water. He was one of the original members of Tammany Hall. His name may still be found on High Bridge in New York City. In his pocket he carried a list of rules for conduct in life, which for years was known as "Stephen Allen's Pocket Piece." It was found in his pocket when his body was recovered from the water of the Hudson. As a child I read the wise and humorous sayings, and unconsciously their truth took root in my soul.

1. Keep good company, or none.
2. Never be idle; if your hands cannot be usefully employed attend to the cultivation of your mind.
3. Always speak the truth.
4. Make few promises.

5. Live up to your engagements.

6. Keep your own secrets, if you have any.

7. When you speak to a person, look him in the face.

8. Good company and good conversation are the very sinews of virtue.

9. Good character is above all things else. Your character cannot be essentially injured except by your own acts.

10. If anyone speaks evil of you, let your life be so that none will believe him.

11. Drink no kind of intoxicating liquor.

12. Ever live (misfortune excepted) within your income.

13. When you retire to bed, think over what you have been doing during the day.

14. Make no haste to be rich if you would prosper. Small and steady gains give competency with tranquillity of mind.

15. Never play at any game of chance.

16. Avoid temptation, through fear you may not withstand it. Earn money before you spend it.

17. Never run into debt, unless you see plainly a way to get out again.

18. Never borrow, if you can possibly avoid it.

19. Do not marry until you are able to support a wife.

20. Never speak evil of anyone.

21. Be just before you are generous.

22. Keep yourself innocent, if you would be happy.

23. Save when you are young, to spend when you are old.

24. Read over the above maxims at least once a week.

Hon. Stephen Allen's Pocket Piece.

—o—

AMONG THE VICTIMS

OF THE

"HENRY CLAY DISASTER,"

(Steamboat destroyed by fire on the Hudson River during the fall of 1853), was Stephen Allen, Esq. an aged man of the purest character, formerly MAYOR OF THE CITY OF NEW YORK, beloved and esteemed by all who knew him. In his pocket-book was found a printed slip, apparently cut from a newspaper, of which the following is a true copy. ☞Peruse it carefully.

—o—

Keep good company or none. Never be idle.

If your hands cannot be usefully employed, attend to the cultivation of your mind.

Always speak the truth. Make few promises.

Live up to your engagements.

Keep your own secrets, if you have any.

When you speak to a person, look him in the face.

Good company and good conversation are the very sinews of virtue.

Good character is above all things else.

Your character cannot be essentially injured except by your own acts

If any one speaks evil of you, let your life be so that none will believe him.

☞Drink no kind of Intoxicating Liquor.☜

Ever live (misfortune excepted) within your income.

When you retire to bed, think over what you have been doing during the day.

Make no haste to be rich, if you would prosper.

Small and steady gains give competency with tranquility of mind.

Never play at any game of chance.

Avoid temptation, through fear you may not withstand it.

Earn money before you spend it.

Never run into debt, unless you see plainly a way to get out again.

Never borrow, if you can possibly avoid it.

Do not marry until you are able to support a wife.

Never speak evil of any one. Be just before you are generous.

Keep yourself innocent if you would be happy.

Save when you are young to spend when you are old.

Read over the above maxims, at least, once a week.

A dusky figure emerges from my memory — the colored butler who for many years superintended the great functions held by the Mayor. Special emphasis was laid upon the New Year's Day reception. Being generous of heart, my great-grandfather had acquired three wives during his triumphal passage through life, and the daughters of these many marriages graciously presided at his receptions when the élite of New York called to pay their respects to the Mayor. Aunt Mary Ann said it was not worth while dressing for less than three thousand, and the beautiful old Coleport punch bowl, large enough for me to drown in, as well as the huge silver cake baskets and the cut-glass decanters, attested to the liberality of my great-grandpa's housekeeping. All the appurtenances of the table were in keeping, and my soul craves for the gorgeous tea service that fed the hosts on those New Year's Days. We are so chaste and colorless in these things now. Whether or not there was any connection between the old colored butler who kept the New Year tradition by calling each year to remind us of his service and receive his due reward, I do not know; but certain it is that a firm of colored men, carrying on a carpet-cleaning business, used the so-called Stephen Allen's Pocket Piece as an advertisement.

My father's father, Homer Foote of Springfield, Massachusetts, was the son of Adonijah Foote, the master armorer of the Water shops of that city, the place where the Springfield rifle was developed. Homer Foote, my grandfather, was apprenticed at an early age to James Scut Dwight, my great-grandfather, a hardware merchant in Springfield. His store was a famous rendezvous. The Boston and Albany stagecoach started at its door, and there forgathered many of the most prominent men of Springfield, the founders of the present Boston and Albany railway.

Among other visitors to Grandfather Dwight's store was his beautiful daughter Delia, and the inevitable resulted. Handsome, gallant Homer fell promptly in love with Delia and shortly after married her. I remember hearing with delight Grandma's story of her first kiss, stolen under the heavy shadows of iron and steel rails, and of the beauty of her fair-haired lover, Homer Foote. He had a remarkable business capacity and in the course of time the business of James Dwight was changed to Homer Foote and Company, under which name it grew to large proportions and became the leading hardware concern of all New England. He became auditor of the Springfield Institution for Savings and a director of the Pynchon Bank.

Added to his ability as a financier, Homer Foote had a fine sensitive feeling for the beautiful. As time brought him prosperity, he built a lovely home for himself on a little hill rising between Maple and

Central Streets in Springfield. This he named Fairview. As a child, I remember he led me out on the verandah to show me the fair view of the Connecticut Valley, and recited to me, in words I never forgot: "I will lift up mine eyes unto the hills, from whence cometh my help."

Music, books, and pictures abounded in his home and there I first learned to love beauty from the canvases of great artists. One of my grandfather's intimate friends was the artist, Chester Harding. He painted portraits of both my grandfather and grandmother. One day at a sitting he said, "Foote, I'm painting a portrait of Daniel Webster. I've got his face all right, but his legs bother me. You're about his size and build. Would you mind letting me paint your legs?" So there hangs somewhere — I believe in the Boston Athenæum — a life-size portrait of the great Defender of the Constitution gayly disporting himself on my grandfather's legs.

If Homer Foote was a merchant and a lover of the arts, he was also a farmer, and long, happy mornings I spent with him and my father at the farm, inspecting the garden, the fruit, and the cattle. My excursions to the farm had elements of humor, some of which might have ended disastrously for me. Papa had an expansive nature. Big men, big endeavors, and the splendid bigness of nature thrilled him. One warm June morning, his soul responding gloriously to the benign influence of nature, he conceived the idea that a sun bath would do me a world of good. Spreading some newspapers under and over me, he bade me lie down in the middle of a strawberry patch. He fed me with a few luscious berries, departed, and promptly forgot my existence in the rapture of a day on the farm. Toward two o'clock I was missed, and then, with some perturbation, they rushed to the strawberry patch, to find a rather groggy little girl verging on sunstroke. I hate to think of what my mother said to Emerson, or what Grandma Allen, usually so mild in her Quaker gentleness, remarked.

Another amusing event. One hot August day, my grandfather Foote and my father attempted to have me look through a sunglass at the sun. Obediently I placed the glass to my eyes, and bravely looked up. It was as if a fiery iron pierced my brain. I dropped it, howling with pain. Papa and Grandpa looked a little sheepish and did not repeat the experiment. Again there were a few poignant remarks, which caused them to lead, for a time, a chastened existence.

My father, Emerson Foote, was his father's second son, one of ten children. He was born in Springfield, April 28, 1837. His mother had so many sisters and brothers that all her children had ready-made names beforehand; Emerson, Cleveland, and Sandford, as well as Francis, Edward, Homer, and James, were named for brothers and brothers-in-law. Papa's education was as curious as it was brief, for at fourteen he graduated from high school and had read six books of Vergil, Cæsar's *Commentaries*, and Cicero's *Orations*, and had a bowing acquaintance with Horace. In after years, his business required learning of sorts, and I never could get over the surprise I felt at his quick mastery of any subject. Banking, mining, patent law, each one was attempted as necessity demanded, and his knowledge always proved adequate to his necessity.

He was active in All Soul's Unitarian Church, holding the treasurership of that organization for many years. Dorman B. Eaton, to whom we owe our Civil Service system, Joseph H. Choate, Peter Cooper, and many other Unitarians were his intimate friends. But in these early days, before I was born, Dr. Henry W. Bellows, the minister, was the object of his affectionate admiration. With him Papa worked in the founding of what was then called the Sanitary Commission of the Civil War, from which the Red Cross developed. My grandfather, William Mortimer Allen, was living at the time of the Civil War on Fifth Avenue near Thirty-eighth or Thirty-ninth Street. I never tired of hearing my mother tell me stories of the meetings of the Sanitary Commission held there. Similar groups, organized by Dr. Bellows, met all over the city.

Mamma's friends would gather in the afternoon

to roll bandages and make dressings. Afterward
the boys of the Seventh Regiment, Company K, of
which Papa and his brother Edward were members, would come in for a waffle supper. Horace
Porter, afterward a general and a well-known diplo-
mat, John M. Wilson, another embryo general, —
both sweethearts of my mother in West Point days
before the war, — came also, and for a time their
hearts were lightened during evenings of homely
pleasures.

Different, however, was the picture she gave me
of the regiments passing down the Avenue for the
front, and the pitiful return when the ranks were
reduced to a handful of tattered and discouraged
men. Each time I pass the Shaw Monument in
Boston, Mamma's description of the splendid
young officers flashes before my eyes. The
sunshine, the courage, the animation as, with
springing step, the most representative of Massachusetts youth passed gayly by. Then the return,
slow and pitiful, of the decimated remainder.

When the Civil War ended, the Union League
Club was another outgrowth of the Sanitary
Commission and for years exerted a powerful
political influence. Papa was a charter member.
During many years the Club was one of the great
pleasures of my father's life, for there he associated
with men of learning, of political importance, as
well as many who represented the world of art and
literature. Papa often spoke of evenings spent

listening to the animated conversation of Mr. Depew, of Mr. Choate, of William Winter, and sometimes of George Smalley, the English correspondent of the *Tribune*. It is impossible to remember the almost interminable list of men — travelers, artists, politicians, lawyers, and writers — who at intervals influenced and enriched my father's life, but of all, Mr. Gawtry, President of the Consolidated Gas Company and my adopted uncle, and Mr. Harris Fahnestock, first President of the First National Bank, stand out as those who were most truly loved by my father, and who most faithfully stood by him as the dark clouds of his later life gathered.

Never will I forget, never cease to thrill, over the remembrance of the cutting of the Thanksgiving cake, in my grandfather Foote's home. Of course all who are New Englanders will remember the pomp and glory of Thanksgiving in those days. The bustle of preparation for days before gradually increased as the great day approached. Not only cakes and pies, but beautiful dresses and marvelous coiffures were prepared. The beautiful old house was cleaned and made to blaze with a kind of benevolent sentimentality as, one after another, members of the family forgathered to take part in the festivity. And the air was over-fragrant with delicious odors of turkeys, ducks, geese, and all kinds of vegetables yielding up their virtues for the feast.

The day arrived. Shades of the departed, where did you get your digestions? Breakfast was a mere trifling meal of an hour or so: hot breads of endless variety, coffee exhilarating by its fragrance, and literally warming the cockles of one's heart, for houses were none too warm and November in New England is a fine month of cold, foretasting winter. There followed fried oysters, chops, corned-beef hash, and griddle cakes, served with loads of butter and cream too thick to be poured.

Then a little silence, and the stately walk to church. Here the festival took on a more solemn tone, and deep and reverent voices raised hymns of thanksgiving to God for His goodness throughout the year. Church over, our hearts were free for another kind of rejoicing. The meeting of friends, the interchange of compliments and experiences, the reawakening of affections dormant throughout a year.

At last approaches the great hour. Thanksgiving dinner is ready. In full evening dress, though it is two o'clock only, my grandparents enter the beautiful blue parlor. The surrounding walls are rich with the paintings Grandpapa loved so well, and soft lights reveal the beauty of his wife and family as, one after another, the children and grandchildren of Homer and Delia Foote arrive to greet their parents on this Thanksgiving Day. Then Grandma seats herself at the piano, and her gouty fingers once more play the music by which for years her children have marched into the dining room for the great feast. Her children and their wives or husbands sit at the large table, while the grandchildren have a table to themselves. Wines of different kinds appear in due order, as the long procession of foods marches by in stately dignity.

About five, a little weary, — and let us hope, not too ill from all the culinary glory, — the family separates, the women not to appear till the evening reception, when Grandpapa entertained all the "sisters and the cousins and the aunts."

The men again meet at seven, and then comes the great moment, the cutting of the Thanksgiving cake. Port and sherry alone accompany this rare and delectable dish, and as the knife separates the cake into rich golden pieces, it is accompanied by the singing of my grandfather and his seven sons. All of them have rich, melodious voices — tenor, baritone, bass. They sing, unaccompanied, only the simple melodies of the people, but with a beautiful feeling for melody and harmony: "Nellie was a lady," "Old Black Joe," "'Way down upon the Swanee River." Perched on my father's knee, I thrilled to the sentiment as well as to the beauty of the festival. In after years it is still a lovely memory. About nine, the family — the big family of all the relatives — began to arrive and more formal music entertained the guests.

It was truly a day of feasting, and I feel that the great joy of the music, the element of thankfulness that inspired us, the vast and generous hospitality that really was a thing of the heart rather than of purse and prominence, all were a legacy of infinite value to me.

When my parents were not at the theatre, opera, or the home of some friend, our evenings were spent in the middle parlor, a room gleaming in a deep red setting, where we chatted or read before a wood fire. Here would gather a few choice friends, and a stately game of whist — the old whist, not the hybrid bridge or auction — would progress. I sat curled up on the sofa one evening, drawing, and a series of rather remarkable boats resulted. Queer gull things, never getting quite into the water, sometimes floating perilously near the moon, but to the discriminating judgment of my parents, always alert for the suggestion of any inclination on my part, here was indicated something to be cultivated. At once began hours of pure delight with a sweet, gentle soul, Miss Alicia Crocker, who gave me lessons in drawing and later in water color.

Busily engaged one day drawing the head of a horse, a certain shape of the cheek baffled me. I drew and erased, drew and erased, and finally, exasperated, seized a heavy black pencil. Before the startled and horrified eyes of my gentle teacher, I took it with both hands and, bearing with all my strength, made a straight hard line wide and heavy enough to all but cut the paper. It was the child equivalent of saying D——, that most helpful of all words ! What rest to a tried and weary spirit that one explosive gives. God, the great psychologist, probably invented it to help His suffering children, and it was a stupid prophet who pronounced as a commandment, "Thou shalt not swear." Of course, I should have been punished. The more intelligent teachers of to-day would doubtless have seen embryonic tendencies of a quite fearful nature in this outburst. But the patient lady beside me, after a mild convulsion of shocked surprise, began the erasing process all over again. The memory is still vivid, for to my restless nature the sustained effort was more than taxing, and every time I look at the amiable face of that horse or speak to the dear patient lady who taught me, visions of that room, the drawing boards, and the half-finished sketch rise vividly before me. Nothing could have been more lasting. Did that long, slow erasing start the self-discipline of after years ? I wonder.

In my mother's home, good housekeeping stood out predominant. You could tell the time of day by what the maid was doing. If Jenny was brushing the fourth step of the front stairs, you could lay your last dollar that it was ten-thirty A.M.; and as sure as it was Thursday night, so did we feast on chicken. Order and method carried to its nth degree — a little of a strain to irregular Papa and me, but excellent for the smooth running of the house. Mamma was a religious woman, but her real God was good housekeeping, and system was

A GROUP OF EARLY FAMILY PICTURES

STEPHEN ALLEN

CATHERINE LEGGETT ALLEN
MARGARET WRIGHT LEGGETT

SARAH ROAKE,
STEPHEN ALLEN'S WIFE

ADONIJAH FOOTE

His handmaiden. Weddings, baptisms, receptions, and dinners were always "of a Thursda'," as Maria, the maid, would say, because the laundry was out of the kitchen. I used to wonder what on earth would happen if any one of us had the temerity to die the latter part of the week. What an upset to the aforesaid Maria if the funeral, instead of the washing, had to be done "of a Monda'." There were elements of humor in my mother's housekeeping.

Being a good mother, she desired a spherical education for her daughter, so at intervals, even in my early days, I spent long, delightful afternoons helping Jane, the cook. Possibly they were not altogether delightful for Jane, but to me my adventures into the realm of home-made pies, roasts, and broils were sheer delight. I having heard Jane say she must "draw" the turkey, and being filled with an honest zeal to assist, Jane's feelings may better be imagined than described when she saw the aforementioned turkey on a long string, being "drawn" over the cold stones of the back yard by literal me.

I smile at times, to-day, as "pasteurized," "modified," and "acidophilous" milk wagons pass me by. The method was far more simple when I was a little girl. Jane, before going to bed, left outside the kitchen door, *on the sidewalk*, a nice old milk pail, and the next morning Borden's man dipped the day's milk, rich in germs if nothing else, out of an open can into the pail, thereby subjecting infant me to every contagious disease the world has ever known. It's a good germ that knows its business apparently, for here I am, sixty years old, having never had any infantile diseases except measles and whooping cough.

Only once were my ears boxed, and that was when the excitement of getting ready for my first opera — *Mignon*, with lovely Christine Nilsson — got the better of me and induced an impertinent answer to a command of my mother's. I remember much hurrying and scurrying to and fro, a sharp command, an impertinent answer from small me, a swift cuff on the ear, and the irate voice of Mamma saying, "There is one thing I won't stand from my children — impertinence." Those were the days when children were taught: "Honor thy father and thy mother."

For punishment, during my father's absence in Europe, I was forced to sit — a little *hard* sometimes, according to the degree of my mother's irritation — on a chair; opposite, on another, was placed my father's photograph; and I can hear the awful tones of my mother's voice say, "Look at your dear father's face. See how sad he is because of your naughtiness." For a dreary half-hour there I would sit. First, as I watched Papa's face it grew sadder and sadder to my infant imagination; gradually tears would fill his eyes and rain in torrents down his cheeks, and then the black iniquity of Jonathan Edward's original sin was actually mild compared with the wickedness I found lodged in my small breast. Reduced to weeping and bitter lamentation, I was finally released amid wild protestations to be a good little girl and never be naughty again. The same picture looks from the wall of my bedroom at me to-day, but now it seems to smile with a tolerant patience at my more mature iniquity.

Religion? Ah, yes, a very real and practical religion, Unitarianism. What do I not owe to it? That faith which, divesting the soul of all its finery, exposes it bare to the critical investigation of the brain. It teaches courage to face life, not for fear of future punishment or hope of ultimate reward, but believing and teaching that God, Who has dealt with us so wisely and tenderly here, can be trusted utterly and entirely in the world to come.

II

READJUSTMENT

I AM always glad to think that my education was, for the most part, informal, and had not the slightest reference to a future business career. It left me free and untrammeled to approach my business problems without the limiting influence of specific training. For my temperament, this was best.

How simple my childhood was, how untheoretical my upbringing, it amuses me now to reflect, when I see present-day parents trying to teach children how to be happy, how to learn. I was happy. I learned quickly. I was let alone. Governesses I had, of course, and schooling, but my little-girlhood was a great simplicity compared to the carefully worked-out daily schedules of modern children. The very fact that I was left free to find my own tastes, suggests the tempo of the life of that time. People had leisure. Life was not interpreted in a great deal of motion, a confusing "busyness." It makes me glad I am sixty instead of twenty, for I cherish the freedom from surveillance which was mine as a child. But the thought of it must give a modern educator gooseflesh.

My grandfather Allen had an extensive library where I was turned loose. No one told me that this or that book was "good for" me. Wide and free was my selection. I was in England shortly after the Wonderland Alice issued from the pen of Lewis Carroll. Edward Lear's *Book of Nonsense* also became part of my possessions. Daily I walked with the Red Queen. Sometimes I swam, like that other Alice, in my own pool of tears, for I was emotional even in those early days. And glad I am, too. Rather a hundred worries than the life of a clam at high water.

From Smollett to Louisa Alcott, from Shakespeare to Shelley, on through the wide fields of literature I ranged, until finally Browning, Emerson, George Eliot, and Spencer gave me a philosophy of life. I can imagine living without food. I cannot imagine living without books.

I realize that the child of to-day is cared for most meticulously according, let us say, to Hoyle — not one little bit according to Heart. I wonder if this is really such an advance over yesterday. My first ten years were singularly happy and care-free. I learned much, but not in the way of books, except that a French governess taught me so well the beautiful language of France that to-day I spell better in French than in English. And an old Irish cook was perhaps my most consistent teacher during this first decade. But there came a time when governesses, French and English, Jane the cook, and John the coachman, were not equal to the further training of Miss Alice, and so to school I was sent. New York was a small intimate place at that time, and there were only three good private schools. Anna C. Brackett's School for Girls was my parent's choice. Its very title is indicative of its policy. Miss Austen had influenced people to speak of girls as "young ladies." Miss Brackett's brusqueness dubbed us by the less elegant title. Those of us who were taught by this marvelous woman still think of ourselves to-day as "Brackett's girls."

We lived on Eleventh Street, and Miss Brackett's was on Thirty-ninth. My walk thither was a triumphal progress. I started at Fifth Avenue and Eleventh, and by the time Twenty-third Street was reached my bodyguard frequently numbered six or eight young boys, intent on relieving me of the burden of my books, bestowing upon me, in the ardor of their youthful affection, sweet nosegays of lovely flowers. Of course I did not know consciously then what fun it was — the jokes, the laughter, the careless merriment of youth, the lovely crispness of the winter's morning, or the spring days making the young men's fancies more poignantly loving than was quite good for any of us. So attractive were these morning walks, indeed, that even on the stormiest days, when slush and snow made rubbers quite useless and no umbrella would withstand the tempestuous wind, I would steal away and walk that long distance instead of riding in the slow-moving, ill-smelling horse car. In those days the floors of cars and omnibuses were covered with the same kind of straw my father used for bedding his horses. Starting off clean, it soon became a sodden mass of mud and filth. Not an agreeable condition to ride in for half or three quarters of an hour. To this I preferred soaking shoes and stockings, and since my dresses reached to my ankles, these too became sodden with muddy water. I did not catch cold or have pneumonia, and when in later years poverty prevented my using the ordinary safeguards against exposure, the experiences of my schoolgirl days stood me in good stead and prevented my yielding to the traditional ideas wrapped around the prescriptions for good health.

To Anna C. Brackett education meant equipment, as well as knowledge and culture. Equipment to face life on its own terms, and give battle, without fear or favor, to its joys as well as sorrows. For to many of us ease is far more soul-destroying than trouble.

In after years I said to her, "How did you do it?" and she said, "Well, you see I had a plan." That was it — a plan, not an experiment. An appreciation of the many and varied calls of life, and a plan to make girls — not young ladies — fit to grapple with vicissitudes and capable of enjoying beauty.

There was no namby-pamby coddling of our

embryo individualities, no palliating of error, no compromise with truth. Our responsibility was fixed. We had no marks, no examinations, but unconsciously we were judged by a jury of our peers, our classmates, and swift, sure, and unerring was their verdict. We had to do our lessons well, or feel their contempt. A far truer standard and more illuminating and practical than bringing home A in arithmetic to dear Mamma. And, by the way, arithmetic was torture to me. All those vile wall papers and carpets that never did fit, and the still more terrible "If John had $12\frac{5}{8}$ apples, and he gave Susie $7\frac{2}{3}$, how many would he have left?" Thank heaven, I don't have to do those hateful miscellaneous exercises to-day. In spite of all life's discipline, I simply could not stand them.

But I did learn my arithmetic tables, upside down, inside out, forward, backward, until I knew them in my sleep and sang them in my waking hours. You see, life is an arithmetic table, and the sooner we learn that fact the better fitted we are for the difficult adjustments it requires of us. If we learn what two-times-two means at five, our extravagance is not so apt to drive our husbands to suicide at forty-five. That is what it is to be educated. To hold our emotions and desires down to the simple facts of two-times-two. Later we may realize, with Emerson, that two-times-two equals five, but that, of course, is another and sweeter story.

My Latin exercises, after they were corrected

with the terrible blue and red pencils of stern Miss Brackett, looked more like Turner's Slave Ship than the modest effort of a schoolgirl. In a course in Greek history Lilian Taylor, Bayard Taylor's daughter, established in our growing souls an abiding love for the Greek and the Great. One hated to be small and petty who walked intimately with Epaminondas, nor could one ever sink in the maelstrom of a dark despair whose soul had thrilled to a Madonna of Raphael or a poem of Shelley. That was education at Miss Brackett's.

Along with school came the daily drill of my patient mother in training me into ways methodical, orderly, careful, and thrifty. Domestic Science was unknown then, except as every woman automatically practised it. Not to be a good housekeeper and seamstress was something of a disgrace in the eyes of my mother's contemporaries. "A place for everything and everything in its place" was one of the most useful lessons ever taught me. To-day my daughter says, "No one on earth, Mother, is as orderly as you are. I just wish you could see other girls' bureau drawers." I dare say; but I know the old saying of a place for everything saved me innumerable hours of "I can't imagine where I put my gloves." Not only is orderliness an economy; it produces rest.

The age of ten was a turning point toward the life of the world. Many things happened to me then. Not only school was added to my experiences, but piano lessons as well. They were almost my undoing, and certainly contributed to a later neurasthenia. I was taught by a friend of my father's, M. Rivarde, a famous musician under whom my father himself had studied. M. Rivarde was an irascible, temperamental Frenchman whose rages never troubled my father one little bit, while to me they were torture. From the all-pervading love of parents and servants, I suddenly encountered, alone and unprotected, the rage of a Latin who knew no self-control, who assumed as a premise that all children were liars, and who had not the faintest feeling of patience, understanding, or sympathy.

Petrified with fear, I went twice weekly to the den of this roaring lion. As his temper began to mount, false notes fell from my fear-frozen fingers like drops of rain in a summer shower. Added to his bellowings were the sharp taps of his ruler — No, not on me; it might have been easier — on the case of the piano, on the marble mantelpiece, on anything hard, metallic, noisy. And all the time the vile regular beat of the metronome, tick-tick, tick-tick. After a lesson I would cry the night through.

Day after day I struggled with those dreadful exercises. Even though doctors warned of the danger to my whole nervous system at that critical age, Papa was deaf. M. Rivarde was his friend, and therefore not anyone in the world could so well teach the piano to his daughter. So the dreary years went on : exercises, scales — scales, exercises. Never a melody to break the monotony for eight years. Imagine my feelings after that time to hear M. Rivarde say, "And bom-by, when we are finished, we will begin all over again."

And yet I could not quite blame Papa, for so much pleasure had been his that he could hardly appreciate anything else connected with his singing maestro. At that time M. Rivarde was quite the rage. Clara Louise Kellogg and Annie Louise Cary were his pupils, singing nightly at the Academy of Music, together with Campanini, del Puente, and Christine Nilsson.

When my fingers had gained sufficient facility, I played my own accompaniments and soon was singing with Papa much of the music of the Italian operas. Then M. Rivarde did scold! What did he mean, the *bête* Monsieur Foote, to let a little girl sing all that high, florid music? Did he want to ruin her voice? But this time Papa disobeyed M. Rivarde quite as casually as he had previously ignored the advice of our physician. So, though I wept at playing, singing dried my tears. Now, in retrospect, the agony of the piano still remains acute and poignant. But as we grow older we learn to "see life steadily and see it whole," and always music has been the solace of my saddest hours.

Then, also when I was ten years old, my brother Emerson was born, and Mamma had to forgo some of the pleasure of her intimate association with my father. To fill this gap, and believing in the great educational value of the play, Papa took me every Saturday night to the theatre. Then indeed was my life enriched.

One's first impressions are so vivid and one's eyes so uncritical, one's enjoyment so intense, that I am perhaps prejudiced, but nothing of to-day seems quite so satisfying, quite so worth while as the comedies played by the stock companies at Daly's and Wallack's. Plays interpreting clearly and without embroidery the low meanness as well as the lofty peaks to which human nature may attain, or plays that merely gave one a few hours of laughing delight. The *School for Scandal*, *School*, *Caste*, Shakespeare in infinite variety, all came to my eager call, answered my insatiable demand for understanding. There were great actors in those days: Booth and Barrett, Salvini, John McCullough, Adelaide Neilson, Modjeska, Mary Anderson, while, as I say, the regular stock companies at Wallack's, Daly's, and the Union Square, gave the best of modern and classical comedies.

Papa would not go to see Sarah Bernhardt because of her immorality. How standards vary with time! Driving up Fifth Avenue one afternoon, Papa took infinite pains to explain to me the difference between bad and good women — the one rouged and powdered. This was the outward visible sign of the black iniquity of her heart and soul, a kind of scarlet letter on lips and cheeks.

When I was very young, girls and boys were kept in ignorance of the sin of the world, and a kind of veil of watchful guardian love was drawn around their growing souls. People did not deem it necessary to parade vice for their benefit. Quite tenderly and very tactfully, Mamma revealed certain secrets to me "when it was time," but she wisely left me greatly to a life of abstract faith in beauty and purity, knowing full well that life itself would soon enough reveal the other side to me. It is not so with our girls and boys to-day. In our desire to clarify the meaning of life for them, we look through a glass darkly.

Those years loitered by filled with many delights. Then came the sinister suspicion of the disaster to my father's fortune. A disaster as terrible to me almost as to him, for my father was my first and perhaps my only great love. Certainly the most enduring. His beauty, his bonhomie, his charming personality, his goodness, fascinated me and drew me to him in a bond so strong, so profound, that to be with him was the greatest joy.

A second son was born to my parents when I was fourteen, Harry — *my* first child, I sometimes think, for all my mother love found in him its first expression. Well worthy was he of all love, all devotion. He inherited many of my father's most lovable qualities and much of his charm. Without any training — apparently my struggle with the piano was sufficient "practice" for all three of us — he played the piano and the guitar most beautifully, while Emerson, my other brother, played the piano and the banjo. We were quite a noisy family, what with our voices and our various instruments.

But while the boys were little, Mamma became more and more engrossed in her household duties, her sewing, and her reading, and I entered ever more deeply into the intimacies of my father's life. He had a genius for finance, and had quickly risen to eminence among the business men of New York in the early seventies. Thus he earned a large fortune, and, being too sure of himself to foresee a possible disaster, was left penniless when it came.

Terrible days of effort followed. The wolf came near our highly respectable door, and Papa went from one mad venture to another in the get-rich-quick hope, only to be baffled, beaten at every turn. And I, his constant companion, shared this misfortune in the blind, uncomprehending way of a young girl, suffering the tortures of a profound sorrow over the incomprehensible trouble of my darling father. Night after night I lay awake, weeping and worrying, unable fully to understand, magnifying the danger, powerless to help, impotent to avert the approaching catastrophe.

My mother grew cold and unsympathetic, Papa's

sunny laughter-loving nature changed to quick, unreasoning irritability, and I, his constant companion, bore the brunt of his carping criticism. Proud of me as the apple of his eye, his very pride caused my misery, for, in a perfectly irrational way, he heaped upon me every form of devotion and ruined all by the irascible outpourings of his over-wrought nerves. I was on a veritable rack. His upbraiding and criticism tore my soul, while my heart broke at the thought of what his reverses meant to him.

Our home became an empty shell. There was the semblance of comfort, there was the music, there were the books, but the soul had gone. Cold contempt had taken the place of love in my mother's and brother's hearts. The radiant sunshine of my father's nature had changed to harassed anxiety. My first great sorrow inundated my soul, and I wandered bewildered and forlorn.

Once again, as in my infancy, my Quaker grand-mother enfolded me within her sheltering love, and what peace I had at that time came when I went to her. She died just before the birth of my first child, but never has she seemed far away. Such love is true immortality.

Fortunately, there has always been a kind of India-rubber quality to my nature, and no matter how hard sorrow pressed me down, back I would spring to laugh, sing, and dance. The world always supplies companions for our gayety at least, so dances and dinners, parties and partners, arrived at regular intervals to lift the dreary gloom of my father's home.

Perhaps it were wiser not to dwell on the too many boys who embroidered my life at this time. Bobby and Walter, Jack and Paul — I wonder if to anyone else they ever appeared quite so beautiful or so noble, so clever or so fascinating as they did to me. They came and went until finally, when I was twenty years of age, Allan MacDougall, the man, my husband, entered.

Fourteen years older than I, ripe in the knowledge of the man of the world, he it was whom God chose to take me far from the circle of love and tenderness, of care and protection, and lead me slowly, painfully, through the dark mazes of dreadful disillusionment, until at the age of forty my life sentence was pronounced.

III

FRONT STREET AND HOW IT GREW

WHEN we were married, on June 14, 1888, Allan was thirty-four — I twenty-one. He was a most successful business man, one of the coming leaders of the lower Wall Street district where the coffee business grew and flourished. Tall, dark, exceedingly handsome, and most popular, the world seemed to invite him to the best it had to give.

But even then the inherent weakness of his nature had begun to sow the seeds of disaster, and little by little complete disintegration followed. Within a short time a change came, incredible to me. No longer was there the smile, the alert address toward the duties of life — rather a slinking, pathetic fear and a slow relinquishment, not alone of responsibility, but of all happiness and joy — heartbreaking to watch, and all but unendurable. I tried to take him into my arms as I would a little child, and love him back to self-respect and manhood, only to realize that the task was hopeless.

Scarcely had I married when some dim premonition of my destiny came to me. The contrast was fearful between the loving, sheltered comfort of my family life and the new, hard, cruel, and unanticipated future. One resolution was born of my despair — I would face life alone as best I might, but I would never bring another soul into a world of torture such as I knew. Yet when my children came, what a joy — what a challenge to live the best that was in me! You see how very much better than I God knew of my necessity, and with what wisdom He placed upon me responsibilities wherewith to triumph.

Gladys, from the moment of her birth, became the epitome of all my love and my ambition. I never allowed a nurse to care for her — never did I leave her. Of course I thought that dolls would be to her what mine had been to me. But no, Gladys had other ideas, and dolls were discarded while her spirit turned to singing and poetry, wanderings among books and flowers. Hers was an accurate soul. One day she said to me, "Is 'well-bred,' toast, Mamma?" I can see her, an elfin sprite, gowned in blue of a summer day's heaven, dancing down a hill toward our little home in Norfolk, Connecticut. The sun seemed to love her golden hair, for it reveled among its curls. The broad red road crept windingly away behind her, and the tall trees bent their loving branches over this darling child of my saddened heart. There was a kind of dancing to the happiness Gladys gave me.

Allan — as I write, each one seems dearer than the rest — Allan was a round-faced, amiable soul from the very beginning, so amiable, in fact, that I all but let him starve to death. The summer in which he was born was one of the most terrible of my life. The heat was intense and Gladys was ill. I never knew quite what happened, but she cried and screamed incessantly unless I held her. No, she was not a naughty child. Long years after, I understood. But there, alone and penniless, I could only minister to her immediate needs, and in caring for her I quite ignored dear, darling Allan, who never cried, but lay in his crib, languid yet always smiling. Then suddenly I realized that he was getting no nourishment from me, and fortunately a quick change of diet saved him to be the joy of my life.

He became an exceedingly vigorous little boy, and I felt that no play would satisfy his active, inquiring mind. So when he was three years old, round-faced, red-cheeked, blue-eyed, and golden-haired, I let him go to a kindergarten. It was the one bright experience of two dreadful years we spent in Englewood, New Jersey. Mrs. Willard, who ran the little school, was one of those rarely intelligent women one encounters at long intervals in one's journey through life. Cultivated, witty, highly developed spiritually, she took the babies of her kindergarten to her heart, and, no matter how young, endeavored to teach them games with a reason — a purpose that related itself to their present needs as well as those of later life.

Even at three, Allan had definite ideas of his own, and he and Mrs. Willard had a battle royal until my glorious son realized that he was part of the kindergarten and that the kindergarten was not a part of him.

A wonderful festival occurred at Christmas when each child said his little "piece." Gladys recited a lovely thing of George MacDonald's; Allan, in his wonderful baby talk that few but I could understand, the following : —

> "Who slays de li'n,
> Who slays de gi'nt,
> Who conquers dem bof however defi'nt?
> De li'n Passion, de gi'nt Sin,
> He conquers, who conquers wiven.
> He can rul'd de worl' who can rul'd his soul,
> And keep himself in his own control."

Being much tried by the long effort, the last line was said very rapidly and became a hopeless jumble of inarticulate words, but the first lines stirred all the dramatic in his nature, and I doubt if Edwin Booth himself could have repeated them with more fiery intensity.

Don came just at the time when my husband's condition had reached its lowest ebb, and when the strain of my awakening to the different responsibilities of my life had greatly reduced my own vitality. He was born at four-thirty in the morning, one cold February day, and about half past seven my angel Allan began the day by showing just how naughty a naughty child can be. No one but me could manage him, so I arose, went to his room, and peace reigned once more in our household. After that there were so many household tasks to see about, so many important things to be done, that I decided it was not really worth while to return to bed as one usually does. When Don was three hours old, I assumed the usual routine of life, and things went on quite as if there had not been the arrival of a little boy.

The strain of my husband's condition, the terrible poverty, the bewilderment in my soul, and the new and utterly unexpected trend of my life, all occupied me so intensely that I was a poor mother for my baby, and I think he has never been so strong as my other children. Calm of soul as well as love of heart on the mother's part is very essential to a little child, I think.

Slowly the truth dawned as I discovered our real situation. Instead of being supported, I must support. Instead of a life of love and tenderness, I must be the one to give tenderness and ask for it no more.

Long, slow, weary months of disillusionment and bewilderment ensued, while the process of development went on to equip me for my real life — the thing, it seems, for which I was born. Dreadful days of doubt, cynicism, fear, began. I lost all faith in God and man. The light went out of the skies — all that was beautiful in life appeared an empty delusion. My sole and only companion was stark, silent, lonely, grim despair.

Once it all but conquered me. We had moved to Englewood just before Donald was born. I remember standing in the bow of the ferry boat one black, cold, midwinter night. The wind howled and the sleet and rain cut my face. Beside me stood the grim, silent, unresponsive figure of the man who was my husband. Slowly I drew nearer — nearer to the edge, intent upon taking the final plunge that would end forever my hopeless misery. And then, before my eyes, appeared two lovely, smiling faces, my baby boy Allan, my little daughter Gladys. I drew back, ashamed of my cowardice, and then and there dedicated myself to the hard but heavenly task of safeguarding them. Within my own heart then I shouldered my burden, faced the unescapable.

During my girlhood money had been easily obtainable. I was never given an allowance. I would return from some festivity to find my purse filled with coins and bills placed there by my indulgent father as a surprise. And for the larger necessities Papa had accounts everywhere. What I wanted I bought and charged. Imagine, then, the bewildering struggle for readjustment. Instead of all the comfortable affluence of my childhood, I was living on a minus sign — and the inevitable followed.

Three months after the birth of Donald the sheriff came to the door with a notice of dispossession. I can still feel my throat contract with the curious terror of that moment. To no one of all the long line of people on either side of my family had such disgrace ever come. It was simply a thing that did not happen to us.

I was upstairs giving my baby a bath when I heard a rude, heavy voice, asking for me. The little maid who assisted me answered the bell. She came upstairs with the message that a man wished to see me. "Ask the man to tell you what his errand is," I said to her, so entirely unaware was I of what *could* happen. She came back to say I must come down or he'd come up. I saw the sly pleasure of the servant in her mistress's distress. I went down, of course, and received one of my first lessons in poverty. I felt so small, so inadequate, as this ordinary man dictated terms to me. He said, "Why did n't you come down the first thing? I could have nailed this notice of dispossession on your house, but I wanted to save you a little of the disgrace." He was chewing tobacco, I noticed with absorbed horror, as he said I had "three days' grace" in which to meet the rent.

It was three days of hell, rather. I had not a penny of money and no immediate means of getting any. I could not even reach my parents by telephone, as our houses had no telephones then. Englewood is small, righteous, and gossipy, so of course the news of our disaster spread. One after another, the tradespeople called to say that not one bit of food would be delivered unless I paid in advance. Finally my father, though sorely pressed himself, came to my rescue, and the demands of the landlord and all the butchers and bakers and candlestick makers were satisfied.

Gravely, then, I faced facts — cold, hard, pitiless. No visible income, no equipment for this life of poverty and self-support; but there were my three — I could not betray them. In some way I must adjust myself to life according to the necessities of my little children and of God's demands.

I taught myself new economies. I learned — how well! — the hard lesson of out-go and in-come. I not only denied myself every luxury, I deprived myself of every possible essential, and reduced life to its lowest terms of the most meagre necessities. One of the most belittling of many economies was having to go without tooth paste. To brush my teeth in the morning with plain water was almost sickening to me.

I sewed, I sang, I became an amanuensis, for whatever I could get. I made preserves and clothes, anything that would bring in a few pennies here and there until such time as my children were a little older and I could be free for larger endeavors. I scraped along in this way for several years until it was more than apparent that the growing demands of my growing children could not be met by any work I could do at home. I simply had to enter business.

Scarcely can I claim the success that eventually came, for all through my life I have been conscious of an all-powerful Wisdom guiding me. A stern and relentless taskmaster is God, but in retrospect so great is the gain, so well worth while the struggle, that one rests in a complete and unquestioning confidence that all suffering represents a far-reaching purpose, which, if pursued bravely and unflinchingly, leads to an all-satisfying end.

On November 23, 1907, I took the definite step that launched me into business. I went out from my little apartment, a lone woman with a big fight ahead of me.

What, precisely, were the conditions of that fight?

I was forty, and the years had taken their toll. Hysteria and insomnia racked me day and night. I had no business training or business knowledge of any kind. My entire capital was $38. My expenses were $250 a month. My assets were three little children.

Why, then, did I choose business instead of a salaried position? To begin with, I was not trained in anything that would enable me to hold even a poorly paid position; and secondly, I believed in grappling with problems, not avoiding them. If I was successful in business, I could care adequately for my children. If I was not, they would be no worse off than they would be with me in a minor position, poorly paid. I took my gamble, for I was always a gambler with Fate, with chance, with good and bad fortune, using as currency only my own imagination, the force of my own temperament, and my determination to win.

I chose coffee because it was a clean and self-respecting business. No friend, however much he might love me, would buy or drink bad coffee. Therefore I knew I would be free from the stigma of charity.

My husband and all his family had been identified with the coffee business, but as jobbers, dealing in green coffee only. At the time of our marriage there were just two prominent grocers in New York, Park & Tilford and Acker, Merrall & Condit. The coffee everyone used, buying it invariably from one of these two firms, was Java-and-Mocha, and my parents followed the usual rule. When I became engaged, my husband roasted small quantities of the rich aromatic coffees of the South and Central Americas and from that time on my family would use no other.

It was so rich and delicious in flavor, so economical and satisfying, that even before we were married I begged Allan to go into this branch of the business and distribute roasted coffee direct to the consumer. He laughed at the idea, but the conviction remained that here was a means of livelihood. When necessity demanded some activity on my part, I decided upon the roasted-coffee business.

Dealers and jobbers in green coffee have to specialize in tasting and testing coffee, an intricate and delicate operation. The Coffee Exchange standardizes the various coffees under various classifications, hard and soft drinking, mild, good and bad roasters, quakery, acid-y, and so forth, and the unit on which coffee is tested is a pan sample or a blue-paper sample, blue paper and blue walls being good backgrounds from which to gain a true sense of the color, form, and general character of coffee in the green, as we say.

Years before my actual necessity arose, some vague premonition of my future must have urged me to ask my husband for the blue-paper samples of the three different coffees used in the blend he made for us. As one humoring a spoiled child, he brought them home one night, and for years I treasured them, hidden on an out-of-the-way shelf in the closet. When the crash came, they had grown so old and so costly as to be quite beyond me in price, but they served their purpose as an indication of the grade and type of coffee I wanted. From them I built my knowledge of coffee. From them I blended my #2 Special, and with that blend I began my business.

Impressions of those first days crowd my memory in bewildering riot.

A gray stormy morning with sleet, snow, and hail beating into my face, a hasty good-bye to my three little children, an admonition to a dull colored woman to "take care of them," — that futile caution, — a swift descent into the foul, ill-smelling subway; a picture in my mind of a balance of thirty-eight dollars on the blue stub in a check book; a vision of the limitless demands of my family for food, clothing, education, health; and somewhere in the jumble of things was "I," straining, gasping, struggling to meet the emergency.

The first three days passed in a mental fog. A small room at 129 Front Street was secured at that spot where I had alighted from the bus on my first visit to Wall Street when I was a small child of five. Here too my husband had had an office.

My experience in leasing this office — merely a dark, ugly room — is typical of business and its methods. The agent for the building was an ambitious young man. One could hardly blame him for increasing the rentals where, when, and how he could. To him the end justified the means, so with suavity and adroitness he offered me a small room and gave the rent as twenty-five dollars a month. In my eager haste to get started I was ready to accept his offer. And then suddenly I remembered that only a short while before the same office had been offered to my husband for twenty. I talked mildly, gently. Was he sure twenty-five dollars was his lowest price? Certainly. It was and always had been. Then I softly resumed: "Strange, for surely you remember when you offered it to my husband about eight months ago for twenty?" It seemed as if it had suddenly grown warm, the gentleman flushed so. He admitted to a trifling error in accuracy and the office was rented to me at the lower figure. Of course it was amusing. It is indicative, however, of the tireless vigilance one must always maintain if one is to succeed in business. It is not unfair discrimination; it is business. It was n't because I was a woman. He would have been twice as sharp with a man. In business everyone is out to grab, to fight, to win. Either you are the under or the over dog. It is up to you to be on top.

With the lease signed, paper was printed with A. F. MacDougall and the address, as letterheads. You see I did not deem it expedient to proclaim myself a woman by my full signature. The telephone company moved with unusual speed in answer to my pleadings and a telephone was installed. My first purchase, a large box or bin in which to keep coffee, reduced my bank balance to thirty dollars.

There was much antagonism to me on the Street. I was a dreadfully ill woman, and the men gave me "six months." At the end of that time they expected me to disappear as unexpectedly as I had arrived, and one could scarcely blame them. I had no credit, no health, no knowledge. How could I but fail?

To make possible my first purchase of coffee, my dear friend, Mr. J. Noah H. Slee, offered to guarantee me to the amount of $500. My second business day was spent going with Mr. Slee and my three little samples from office to office to make my initial purchase of coffee.

I remember the cold, critical expression in the eyes of the man I first approached, peering at me with antagonism mixed with curiosity through the heavy-lensed glasses of nearsighted eyes. It was wise for me to buy from this firm, for they knew the grade and style of coffee my husband had blended for our home use, and when he refused to have anything to do with me, Mr. Slee demurred. Why should he not sell me? My money was as good as anybody else's. Why discriminate? But I was proud. I knew what I was going to do. I was sure of myself. I drew myself up to my full height of four feet ten inches and said, "My dear Mr. Slee, I think my whole business now and forevermore with Mr. So-and-So will be to wish him a very good morning." Figuratively I had given him a slap on the face I felt he richly deserved. I still see his curiosity change to astonishment. I still hear Mr. Slee say, "What on earth will you do now?" I, however, was not so filled as he with consternation. Then, as always, I relied on myself. And because I believed in the goodness of human nature, I quickly turned my footsteps to the store of W. J. & E. H. Peck. To Mr. Walter Peck I told my story. Kind of heart, impulsive, generous, he opened his stock to me and for at least three years all my coffee was bought from him. Into an out-of-the-way corner of the upper floor of his building I went, and there, away from the trading going on below, I learned tasting and testing, and purchased the coffee I needed for my growing business. I never felt the necessity of returning to the nearsighted gentleman. People without vision are rarely profitable acquaintances.

With only thirty dollars capital I scarcely could afford a stenographer, and again Mr. Slee helped me. My third business day was spent in his office — of the "3-in-1" Oil Company — where the best stenographers took my dictation. I dictated and issued five hundred letters to friends and relatives, explaining my trouble and my great necessity, telling of my plans, and saying, "Will you buy your coffee from me, and, if you like it, speak of it to your friends?"

Harry, my brother, gave me the first order of five pounds; ten friends ordered ten pounds each. Thus began my business.

I established for myself basic principles. I would ask no favors. I would buy nothing until I could pay for it. I would never buy anything until I had to. My office was a dreary place, a small rectangular room with yellowish walls and dull brown woodwork, back from the street and without sunlight. In this I placed my coffee bin. One large packing box served as a desk, another as a chair. Naturally it more or less scratched my knees. It was n't comfortable, but it served its purpose. I bought a few ledgers, sales books, and so on. Mr. Slee gave me a beautiful Venus pencil until I could accumulate wealth enough for pen and ink. My letterheads arrived; my daily programme was arranged.

I always think of the *Bab Ballads* as applicable to me in those days: —

> Oh, I am a cook and a captain bold
> And the mate of the Nancy brig,
> And a bo'sun tight, and a midshipmite,
> And the crew of the captain's gig!

For I was owner and possessor of this wonderful business, its stenographer, typist, bookkeeper, shipping and receiving clerk. Errand boy as well. In the morning I opened my mail, — sometimes I had all of five letters, — ground, packed, and shipped what orders I had, wrote up my books, and bought coffee. In the early afternoon I attended to my correspondence and sent out my daily hundred letters, advertising my business. These letters "pulled," as they say, and to them I attribute my start. I thanked every person who ordered from me, told him or her how much direct help the order was to me, and how honestly I would in return attempt to meet their needs in coffee quality. Seven o'clock and I would start up Wall Street to deliver three or four orders in the residential quarter of the city. That was hard work. Twenty pounds weigh always twenty pounds, but when one is weakened by that horror, nervous prostration, it seems a hundred, and my progress up Wall Street to the subway or elevated was punctuated by stops to hold on to a railing and catch my breath, or to rest my hands from the cutting twine.

Another episode, but of a little different character, imprinted itself indelibly on my mind.

Many of our friends lived on Madison Avenue, and there I used to go, before my business life, to the many teas and receptions given by them. But errands of a different nature carried me there at the time of which I write. One afternoon, when a reception was going on in the home of a long-time friend, I arrived at her basement door weighed down and exhausted by the heavy package of coffee I had to deliver. No one answered my ring, so I entered to escape the too friendly interest of the chauffeurs outside. Inside was much hurry and bustle. Excitable French waiters rushed to and fro with steaming urns of coffee or kettles of boiling water. Maids, anxious-faced, washed plates or arranged creamed dishes and salads. The cook, a large pleasant-faced woman, stood rather helplessly in front of the kitchen table. It seemed to me that she should have been glad to be released for a little while from the arduous cares of stove and refrigerator. But, no, long years of training had made her forget how to be free, just as the rest of us forget how to vacate ourselves of responsibility. As I advanced to the table, a look of questioning surprise overspread her rather glistening face, then a little resentment. But as I explained my errand a sweet expression of sympathetic understanding came, and a quiet feeling of friendliness returned to me.

Outside the chauffeurs grinned and chatted about this unusual type of delivery girl. Embarrassment and a sense of the unreal overwhelmed me. I hurried by. I wonder if college professors realize that the young girls of their classrooms must anticipate this type of business experience if they contemplate commercial life.

Storms in New York, as elsewhere, do not wait on my convenience or anyone else's. One night, typical of many others, I remember well. I had left Front Street at about 8:30 P.M. to deliver coffee far up in the West Side of the city, a district quite unfamiliar to me. I emerged from a subway station approximating my destination, faced into a blinding snowstorm, and, wading through drifts, weighed down by my ten-pound package of coffee, I finally arrived. Returning, I found Allan, then seven years old, looking on Broadway for me, anxiety in his childish face, because I was so late. The smile of welcome he gave me was perfect compensation.

After such a night I would have to go to bed immediately; but usually, after an hour or so with my children, singing or reading to them, as I had always done before going into business, I would put them to bed and then sit at the sewing machine for a few hours more to make their clothes. I had a distinct feeling of triumph when I completed a set of warm woolen pajamas for Allan between eleven and two. When one has nerves one cannot sleep, so sewing was quite restful. Finally, toward morning, I would take some kind of sleeping medicine and forget — it could hardly be called sleep — for a little. At six I was up again, for I had to start the day for my children and order their meals, and my hour for arrival at Front Street was 8 : 30.

Not long after my lease began, I made the acquaintance of poor Jennie, the charwoman; a frail, emaciated creature, she walked with a terrible limp, for one leg was much shorter than the other. She was an Italian and I soon learned to know and really to love her. Joseph, her husband, worked in a basket factory while John, their adored son, was still at school. They had very, very little money. For cleaning the offices Jennie got four dollars a week and, as porter in the factory, Joseph got little more. John sold papers after school hours and eked out their scanty income with a few pennies earned in this way. Jennie talked quite freely, and when I asked her how she got along, she said, "Vel, Mrs. Macca Douga', ve go slow, ver' slow!"

I believed her. But she seemed happy. Her love for her husband and Johnnie seemed compensation enough for her.

One evening she came in to me quite breathless, a wild, hunted look in her brown eyes. I asked her what the matter was. "Ah! Mrs. Macca Douga' — they have gone to the hospital." And then it turned out that Joseph, her husband — there were no singular pronouns in the difficult English language for Jennie — had gone to the hospital for a serious operation. This was bad enough, but she must pay sixteen dollars a week for him.

Poor thing, how easily I understood her terror and how keenly could I sympathize with it! Illness was a terror to my soul too at this time. So I went to the hospital and arranged things. Jennie became once more serene, for Joseph was made well, and things, though still "slow," were not so bad. Then one night, as I sat working after the roar of Wall Street had ceased and I was quite alone, the door of my office suddenly opened and the three, Jennie and Joseph and John, stood in martial array before me, Joseph and John, rosy cheeked and well fed, Jennie the shadow of a woman speaking volumes in self-sacrifice in contrast to the robust males of her family. White with terror, she, the wife and mother, handed me an envelope. "Look, look, Mrs. Macca Douga'," she said. In it I found a bill for $150 for Joseph's long illness. Terror was hers, not alone at the thought of how to pay the bill, but at the hideous danger of imprisonment if she did n't.   In Europe, where Jennie had come from, there is little hope, if any, for the poor if their bills are unpaid.   It was simple for me to reassure her and quiet her fears. A trip uptown, an explanation to an understanding and sympathetic hospital superintendent, so that he adjusted what was but a bookkeeping error, and sunshine crept again into dark 129 for all of us.

Gradually I became established.   Six months had passed, and in spite of the dismal croakings of the coffee men I was still there.   My mail contained perhaps ten daily letters now.   Orders increased; a tiny, tiny spot of the earth's surface was mine.   People knew that A. F. MacDougall was selling good coffee at a reasonable price.   Some knew that there was a woman behind that ambiguous name, honestly trying to support herself and her family, and the great kind world reached out friendly hands and hearts.

Still, it was not easy.   I was dreadfully lonely. Day after day passed and my sole companions were a little Irish stenographer and a Jew who took the strain of the packing and shipping off my shoulders. It took strength, self-discipline, to leave my children alone all day, and day after day; also it was hard to deny myself all pleasure and luxury.   I had almost no time to read.   I could not afford the delights of theatres and music.   To add to my sorrow and loneliness was the separation from my father, who had died just two months to the day after I went into business. With him went a great sustaining and inspiring love; his death came when I most needed him. Sometimes wild despair would overtake me, and a terrible hysteria which tormented me would not be controlled. Hastily flinging on hat and coat, I would rush out. Walking through the laughing lunch-hour throng on lower Broadway, I would rally myself by repeating: —

"One who never turned his back but marched breast forward,
    Never doubted clouds would break."

When quiet returned I would go back to my office to resume my battle.

As I have said, I had no equipment. What thrills when my first chair arrived — a brand-new secondhand one of "antique" oak! Much the worse for wear, but at least a chair. Mr. Peck loaned me a little desk. No place for papers, no convenience, but a genuine comfort not to have my knees continually bruised by the packing-box-desk of my beginnings. And here hours at a time I sat and figured out my small profits and tried to dovetail into them the expenses of my home.

What if I were wrong? If my profit were wrongly computed, then farewell to my whole scheme of life. There was no bliss to my kind of ignorance, I assure you, and long hours of figuring every remote contingency and every immediate possibility made an exhausting addition to the busy day.

Long after Wall Street had put up shutters and gone home, I sat at my bookkeeping, utterly weary, terrified by the loneliness of the dark, silent building, figuring, figuring.

When I had been in business a few months, I found it so very difficult to carry it on with no money that I determined to borrow some, so I explained the situation to my friend Mr. Spalding, who sent the auditor of A. G. Spalding & Bros. to verify my statements. Incidentally, from him I learned all that I now know about bookkeeping. Finding that my own books, while dreadfully feminine and erratic, were in the main correct, he and Mr. William Barbour guaranteed me up to one thousand dollars at one of the large city banks. The arrangement was that I should pay this back to the bank when and how I could. I could never have any more, but I might draw up to that sum — an ineffable boon when people did n't pay their bills and my own matured.

All went along smoothly until on two different occasions, on balancing my account, I found myself short. The first time I was not greatly concerned, but I was, the second. I had no corresponding stub in my check book for either shortage, and the bank returned no voucher for either. Instead of my having — let me say — one hundred and fifty dollars on the second occasion, the bank said I had only one hundred and thirty-five. I nearly wore the paper of my check book out trying to find my mistake. Hours and hours were spent racking my brains to remember cashing a check outside, which I might have failed to enter on my return to my office. I knew I had n't done this — money was too precious and my bank account too small to admit of any such carelessness. Finally I spoke to the cashier. Indulgently he listened — of course it was money paid over the counter. Tolerantly he explained *my* error, and I felt all the humility of a mere woman in the face of men and money. But I was unconvinced, and after spending more weary hours trying to find my error, I wrote the bank that since they could not produce the vouchers, I thought it was poor banking to allow such a thing to happen; that it was not the amount of money involved that disturbed me, but the dependability of their organization. This, to one of the most conservative banks in New York!

Immediately they wrote back that I might withdraw my account if I was not pleased. It was evident that they intended their letter to be a rebuke, not a stimulus to action on my part, but within two hours after the receipt of their letter I did withdraw my account. I transferred my tiny sum, my life raft, to a safer place. The new, friendlier bank now has whatever advantage may accrue from its handling of the banking affairs of a two-million-dollar business annually.

The troubles that beset me were not alone from my own ignorance or need or timidity. Things quite beyond my sphere of influence still affected me. One hot Saturday in August 1909 I worked late, figuring, planning, writing. I was pleased. I was carrying several grades of coffee. Cocoa had made its permanent addition to my stock, and many delicious blends of tea. Orders were increasing and anxiety diminishing. Rest and peace were approaching.

I went home to my restful Sunday duties with a feeling of content. Monday morning, and what a complete change! A bear movement had been started, the market had broken, all values had altered, and the established rest of Sunday was changed into the pandemonium of a disordered market.

Another time the strike of the express companies turned things upside down for me, and made me exercise all kinds of ingenuity to make deliveries, when all delivery had stopped. But in spite of the deterrents of one kind or another, the business pushed steadily forward.

Thus time passed. By November 1909, just two years after my beginning, I was established. My business was about $20,000 gross a year, but the profit in this was small. On each pound the net profit was about four cents. My children were occupied at school throughout their day. Something like security entered my mind. Still I was financing my apartment on a minus sign.

I had established for myself the inviolable rules

mentioned before of paying cash for everything, not only as an excellent policy, but to secure the cash discount. On the other hand, I had to extend credit. Boards of Directors meet at stated intervals and bills are not passed for payment till they do meet. So it happened that two or three months might have to elapse between my payment for green coffee and a rich and luxurious club's payment of my bill. In the interim, unspeakable anxiety for me, sleepless nights of fear and doubt, days of utmost endeavor, a few dollars here to quiet an insistent butcher, saving, saving every little penny to meet the onrushing of my next bill for coffee. Rigid economy, patching, darning, mending at home. Economy of the most careful kind exerted with ever increasing vigor in the office. Look after the pennies, and the pounds — there were no pounds, not even dollars; so pennies here and pennies there saved and multiplied, and life proceeded, and the years passed.

I look back with amusement upon my economies, more especially because they are ingrown and hard to dispense with now when they are unnecessary and have in fact become almost a luxury. For years I cut open each envelope and used the inside for memoranda and figuring. As time passed, my clerks were taught the same method, and as the mail increased we had ample paper for the entire force. Consequently I never spent one penny for paper of any kind except the absolute essentials in letterheads, billheads, and the like. It costs me quite a pang to-day to see my precious envelopes thrown intact into the scrap baskets when we have become so vulgarly, carelessly wealthy and when time is too precious to justify their use.

My apartment was blessed with an open fire, the epitome of luxury to me. After a devastating day of business care, what delight to draw near to its restful, comforting warmth with the children and either read, sing, talk, or sew. And here another economy gladdened my soul. For my tea chests accumulated, pretty in their gay covering of Oriental paper, chests which contained the aromatic teas I used in making my blends. These broken into pieces served as kindling and added to the pleasure of my fire by the spicy sweetness of the Oriental wood.

These economies were trifling in themselves but, multiplied in hundreds of different ways, really accomplished something, except — I blush to think of it — for the offsetting extravagances, which were mainly responses to heart appeals from other suffering souls whose need seemed greater than my own. By what names did I not call myself when it was over and I had to meet the daily demands of my home with more faith than cash !

One of my enforced economies was going without sweets. I longed for them, I craved the stimulant they give. It was a subconscious craving for alcohol in those days of heavy strain and little physical strength. Well did I grow to understand the feelings of the man who took a pick-me-up under mental strain. Years of inexorable self-discipline made me abnormal in my attitude toward food; I still am so. A fifteen-cent malted milk with two crackers made a full meal for me in those days, until one day at the soda counter I saw the sticky mass from which the clerk dipped the syrup he put in my concoction. To cap my disgust and revolt me permanently, he stuck his thumb in the egg as he broke it on the edge of the glass from which I was to drink. That was the end of that sort of midday meal. The only alternative for me was one of the quick-lunch places where about two thousand people eat at noontime, with all the unbearable clatter and confusion. I would wait until 2:30, when the place was rather empty, and ordering a piece of toast, sit down for a dreary moment. Perhaps this is one of the reasons that I years later developed restaurants that are a haven from the blare of the street and the too-great intimacy with one's fellow man.

For my children, however, at this time as at all others, I planned meals that should be nutritious, have an endless variety, and eliminate any waste. I made my menus weekly so as to utilize the leftovers. I used nothing but the most substantial and wholesome foods, but I presented them to the children excellently cooked and in such varied ways that their appetites never flagged and they were always well nourished. Roasts of beef did full-time duty for us. Five meals at least out of a ten-pound roast before submitting the bones to the soup pot, where the left-over vegetables of many meals gave it the delicious flavor I wanted and a little rice or barley added to its nutriment. When the roast behaved in this capable manner, it was simple to recruit the remaining meals from the fish market or use the many less expensive but wholly delicious foods.

Planning thus, I quickly knew to within a few pennies the exact cost of my living. Rent, gas, wages, food — so much a day, so much a month.

In the office I knew with equal surety the profit on each blend of coffee, each grade of tea and cocoa. I devised my "slips." These were narrow pieces of paper — the insides of large envelopes. I multiplied each day the profit (gross) of each blend of coffee, etc., by the number of pounds sold. From this total I deducted my daily expenses, so each evening before going home I knew whether I had made or failed to make enough to pay my running expenses. And this method, primitive as it was, kept clearly before my mind just where I stood. I was encouraged when business was good, curbed when my optimism led to extravagance and the day's slip registered a minus quantity. Above all was the dominant rule to buy nothing that was not an absolute necessity, and not to buy that necessity until I had money to pay for it. To be sure, my nature, which is that of a gambler, led me to take long chances. But courage and ingenuity usually came to my aid, and in the long run worked to my advantage.

And I asked no favors. People have a tendency to boast of their ability and then run to cover like rabbits when a crisis comes, or else seek protection under some stronger intellect. I am like the rest of my kind, and probably would do the same were it not for one thing: I know that in the long run it just does n't pay. Human nature is dear, beautiful, and long-suffering. It reaches out in pity its generous kindness to all who are in trouble, but after all, each one of us has his own responsibilities, and after a while our kindest friend must leave us to work out his own immediate problem. Besides, I could not square it with my own self-respect. So I adopted the principle that I would ask no favors. Perhaps this is not quite an accurate statement, for I had no compunction in draining to the last drop the cup of wisdom and ability in my friends. Did I want some light on advertising, up I went to Mr. Slee. Did some problem of financing confront me, Mr. Walter Spalding shed the sunlight of his powerful brain upon it, and it vanished in thin air. If I were tortured by the vast debates of my soul, the courageous philosophy of Emerson and Browning inspired me for each day's work. But to ask anyone actually to do one little thing for me — that was impossible.

One day Mr. George F. Baker telephoned me and asked me to come to his office. Loving him very dearly and respecting him for his lifelong friendship for my father, I had purposely avoided acquainting him with my trouble. But a mutual friend told him about me and in consequence he called me to his office. I went to the First National Bank — that great bank of a great city. As I entered, what thoughts crowded to my mind of its infinite power and my impotence. We talked together, I knowing full well what was in Mr. Baker's heart. He was embarrassed, I think, for he had all the hesitancy in the world as he said, "Alice, what can I do for you?" and I replied, "Mr. Baker, I don't think there is anything in the world that you or anyone else can do for me. I have a big fight ahead. It is my own special battle and I must fall or rise according to my ability." I believe in burning one's bridges. I believe the only way to conquer is to walk where the battle rages most fiercely, and fight, fight, fight until you win.

It is this kind of determination that man has acquired through long generations, and the woman who is to conquer in the business world must acquire it too if she is to succeed.

Mr. Baker, however, was not satisfied. Those were the days when I was hanging on to life by a rather slender thread. Just as I arose to go, a clerk appeared in answer to Mr. Baker's ring. A thousand dollar bill passed from his hand to mine, so overwhelming me that I all but fainted. I deposited it quickly, minding Mr. Baker's gentle admonition, "Now, Alice, be careful not to lose that," rushed to my office, drew checks for every outstanding bill I owed, and that night slept soundly for the first time in many years.

I could not write of this early stage of my business without remembering Dr. Devan and the *Tribune* Fresh Air Fund. Dr. Devan preached no special theory of life, but his whole soul was dedicated to usefulness, coupled with a wise understanding, with great love and sympathy for suffering, and he gave me the entire order for coffee used at the various camps of the Fresh Air Fund. One morning, early in spring, I called to get my order, and Dr. Devan said, "Mrs. MacDougall, if there is anything else on that list that you think you can sell me, you may do so." I looked over the list of groceries and suddenly noticed that for every pound of coffee there were about five of cocoa, so I said, "I would like to sell you cocoa." "What do you know about it?" "Nothing at all, but this is February. You will not need any till June, and by that time I will know all that is necessary."

From that day and for many after, cocoa salesmen led a weary life and my digestion all but passed away, for I tasted cocoa sweet and cocoa bitter; cocoa fair and cocoa most indubitably foul; cocoa made with xxxx sugar, and cocoa less proud, sweetened with God alone knew what. But by

June large drums of cocoa, as well as bags of coffee, went to the Fresh Air Fund, and I had the satisfaction of knowing that I had lowered the price, bettered the quality, and supplied the little children of the New York slums with a pure and helpful drink.

Twenty years have passed. We still supply them, and not once has there been a complaint of either quality or flavor.

So far all advertising and soliciting had been done by mail. Now, however, I felt urged to greater endeavor and I made my first attempt at commercial traveling.

I had decided upon a direct-to-the-customer mail-order business, but the individual consumer had a quite annoying way of going South in winter and to Europe in summer, and I soon turned to those comfortably all-the-year-round propositions: institutions, clubs, hotels, hospitals, and colleges. At first I did not fare far from home. Money was scarce and traveling expensive, so I zoned a district to a radius of about seventy-five miles from New York and found enough to do to cover the sanitariums and hospitals and other institutions therein.

There was a very well known sanitarium in the outskirts of New Haven, and that journey I remember with vivid distinctness. Arriving at the station, I looked for some kind of conveyance to carry me to my destination. A rather queer-looking man approached me, the type one would call a "character." Old, with gray hair that waved a little as it escaped from a worn fur cap worn jauntily on one side, corduroy coat and waistcoat, and gay check trousers. He asked if he could be of any assistance. I told him what I wanted and he said if I could wait a "jiffy" he would return with a team of "the prettiest pair of Kentucky-bred mares you ever laid eyes on." My love for horses carried the day and in a few moments my debonair Jehu arrived and I found myself seated beside him in a narrow racing road-wagon.

We started. My companion immediately began a rapid-fire conversation. It was early spring. The ground was soft and as we got farther and farther away from the little town, deep ruts lined the road and the wheels sank in while the pretty horses tugged at the traces. There was a lovely sweetness to the air. I was tired and it was good to get away from dirty, noisy New York. I would have been glad to drive in silence and rest my jaded soul. But — no hope; my companion talked and talked, and in spite of my laconic answers, a stream of words flowed ceaselessly into my ears. Having exhausted his fund of anecdotes, he began to recite poetry, edging, little by little, nearer and nearer to me till it seemed as if I was seated on the rim of the wheel.

We were now out in the open country. Fields just beginning to turn green after their long winter's sleep stretched out to the horizon or else reached to the low-lying hills far away. Not a vestige of a house, no sign of a human being. A cow even would have been a welcome sight, for I was beginning to suspect something and felt a bit uneasy.

Then the gentleman stopped the horses, and pressed close to me and began to make love. His horrid breath heated my cheeks. I was conscious of his face coming closer and closer to mine. Disgust — there is n't a word in the English language strong enough for what I felt. The whip was in the socket. I seized it. Words are often useless things, but the words I used, the whip held near the lash with the butt-end free, the look in my face, carried some idea to the beastly creature and he desisted. I did not get to the sanitarium nor have I ever tried to return. He turned his horses about and we drove back to the little town. Any woman can imagine my relief when I saw the train arrive to carry me back to wicked New York. Thus one business episode ended.

That was all it was, an episode of a business day. It did me no harm. I laughed over it the next day and for many months after would recite part of the poem, "The White Goblet and the Red," that had been recited with so much fervor by my amorous companion.

This is the kind of thing that happens to women in business. This is the price one pays for emancipation — it is scarcely worth while, it seems to me. Perhaps because I am mid-Victorian.

Commercial traveling was vivid and lonely and depressing and thought-provoking. My first selling trip to Scranton comes to my mind in scenes, reeling slowly as the hours passed then, midnight till dawn, dawn till noon, noon till night. At midnight in mid-winter I left my apartment and said good-bye to my children. Dress suitcase in hand I climbed the Elevated stair and started for Scranton by the D. L. & W. How small and lonely I felt, going out into the night and the cold strangeness of that journey to parts unknown!

Arriving early the next morning, I breakfasted at a counter, perched on a high, uncomfortable stool, my feet barely touching the rail. My companions were railroad laborers and train hands. I hated the stale, overnight odors of food and the heavy smell of pipe and tobacco of the brakeman who ate next to me. A swallow or two of coffee and I rushed for the fresh air, and rode back and forth over the hills of Scranton till I could go to hospital, club, and hotel and beard the mighty steward in his den.

Nine was the earliest time permissible to call. The interim had to be filled with these solitary but fascinating rides through towns just awaking after a long night's sleep.

And filled with fanciful romance were some of these street journeys. There is always a fascination connected with the awakening of a city. One thinks of the night before and its possible and varied activities, not all bearing the light of investigation very well, and watches with quiet amusement the slow awakening of some houses, while others are quick and alert to greet another day. It is fascinating too to listen as the noise begins, first with the jangling of the milkman, the slow clump-clump of his sleepy horse and the tinkle-tinkle of the milk bottles. And then, one by one, slowly and sleepily but ever yet a little more briskly, other carts in succession, and finally the slow, plodding footsteps of the first early artisans walking to work. In summer it is sweet to listen to the same awakening of life among the birds in shrubs and bushes. In Scranton and Wilkesbarre it was the miners going slowly to work that fascinated me. There had been a heavy snowfall. The streets were narrow pathways. The little places in front of the still dreaming homes were piled high with fleecy snow, while tiny lights blinked like nearsighted old men through their snow-rimmed windows at the rising sun. And then the streets began to fill with the poor, tired, worn-looking miners, black splotches on the breast of the newly fallen snow. In the dull gray of the morning they had a weird, unreal appearance, slouching along with their queer, bulgy, bagging black clothing, their little lamps, dull and useless, fitted into their tight caps.

I felt a prayer creep into my heart and a keen sense of pity for these toilers of the deep places.

Who knew their suffering, their struggle, or at what moment death, far from the cheer of the sun, might reach them?

The Moses Taylor Hospital in Scranton was the goal of my ambition. The superintendent was said to be a cold, reticent woman. People warned me against her as I inquired my way. Finally, when I was shown in, I was quite shaken by fear. A long, nerve-racking wait ensued. At last she came and listened in silence to my selling talk, unsmiling, imperturbable. I was in despair. My long journey and tremendous outlay were useless, my effort abortive. Then to my astonishment, without comment, she drew an order pad to her, wrote out and handed me an order for four hundred pounds of coffee and two hundred pounds of cocoa. I nearly fainted. She gave me not an order alone, but a promise, faithfully kept, of all her subsequent orders. This alone justified the frightful expense of the trip, and encouraged me for my visit to Wilkesbarre and onward. Even then it was hard not to turn tail and run away, so great was my distaste for this personal solicitation, but I was in most cases received courteously, almost always secured the order or business I was after, and always returned with that fine sense of accomplishment, the greatest reward for a self-fought battle.

In selling to hotels and clubs I had generally to deal with the steward, and no one was more difficult, no one took more out of me and my none-too-great strength. One late afternoon I went to the top of a skyscraper on Wall Street to sell coffee to the steward of a gentlemen's club. He was a foreigner. Maybe he was a nice man — I certainly did n't think so as he locked the door and I sat in his little cubbyhole of an office, our knees almost touching. A sardonic smile was on his lips. His small black eyes glistened in a quite tormenting way, and for several minutes he plied me with questions, personal and impertinent. Temper, not courage, came to my rescue. Either I was to dominate or he. The debate did not last long. Having received the order, I departed. I was conscious of breathing a little hurriedly as he unlocked that hateful door and I knew I was free. But it was good — and an experience. I had learned a lesson and secured a customer as well. The next time found me better equipped.

But if this one was irritating, how amusing was the steward of a large New York hospital. Here was self-righteousness on a pedestal. He knew the whole decalogue of morality. No hesitancy was his. No delicacy restrained the mighty onrush of his majestic will. Through a doctor, he knew all about me, and with colossal assurance told me just what I should and should not do, recounted my sins, past, present, and to come, and breathless, demanded why I should ask him to help me. For the first, last, and only time I longed to be a pugilist. I would have loved to make marmalade of his rosy countenance. Then the humor of it all came to me, also the cold commercial value of his order. Bottling up my wrath, I remembered that "molasses catches more flies than vinegar." My lips became saccharine sweet, I gently dallied with my inquisitor, while extolling the virtues of these lords of humanity, the noble company of apostolic stewards. After all, was I not a woman above all things and with three children to support? My coffee was good, my price reasonable, my service excellent. Could n't he? He could. Would n't he? He would and did. Subsequently we became quite good friends.

But these unpleasant encounters were the exception. Never shall I forget the soothing help that came to me after a long, tiresome day in Springfield. Feeling a kind of proprietary right in the town of my father's boyhood, I made it one of my first objectives. It is a large, lovely city, and I went all day from place to place, hospital to hotel, and finally reached the Nyasset Club and Mr. Donald MacDonald. Maybe the Scotch merit their reputation, but in Mr. MacDonald I found a soul generous in understanding, liberal, and without prejudice. Regularly, for many years after, my coffee and tea went to the Nyasset Club. If the membership glowed in a new brilliancy, it was due, I firmly believe, to the coffee supplied by A. F. MacDougall.

After each business trip I returned, exhausted,

and worked in the quiet of my office until again duty summoned me to a new departure in some untried field. It was always the same story. Fear, hesitancy, inadequate physical strength, but will conquering and courage assisting.

One really delightful memory rises from the rather drab background of these trips. Colleges and fraternity houses now became the object of my endeavor. After a busy day wandering around Williamstown, an undergraduate asked me to dinner at his chapter house. Thirty boys, hungry, not alone for dinner but for the things their mothers gave them, circled me at table, and later around the blazing fire. They sang with their strong young voices the delightful college songs. They plied me with a thousand questions, for life was serious and their brave hearts were realizing a little of the gravity of the Great Adventure. Mid-years were over, but finals were not far away, and soon the inevitable "What shall I do with it" would have to be answered by each and every one. How glad I was for the assurance I could give! If I, an untrained woman, broken in health, could meet life's challenge and conquer, what possible chance of failure for them?

But if I succeeded with men and men's undertakings, how dismal was my failure when I approached those institutions designed solely for women's benefit, and officered principally by women!

Explain the antagonism women showed me, as you will, members of the suffrage and feminist movements. I cannot. All I know is that while men sprang ever ready, ever chivalrous, to put business in my way, sometimes even when competitors, women almost invariably turned me down. There were exceptions, of course, as in the case of the superintendent of the hospital in Scranton, and in Martha Van Rensselaer, that amazing woman of the Department of Home Economics in Cornell. There were many exceptions among the hundreds of women housekeepers who were ready and eager to help me get on my feet. But Smith College, Bryn Mawr, the Women's Exchanges, and hundreds of other similar institutions for women were impossible, and in them only I had to admit defeat.

If their hesitancy could have been attributed to the quality of my coffee I would have been the first to acknowledge it. But by the time I approached places like these I was more or less of a specialist. I knew my market, both wholesale and retail. I knew the needs of these people, as my success elsewhere proved. The difficulty — an honest conversation proved that — lay in the quality of the feminine mind. The subtle flattery of an adroit salesman pleased them and their order in consequence went to him. Fear, also, in a dim, unrealized way of those "higher up" crushed their initiative, and I pitied them. But my admiration of college intellect outside of scholastic matters had a severe blow, and my opinion concerning women in general and a certain type of college woman in particular was strengthened.

Even while I deprecated the suffrage movement, I felt that I must turn it to my own account. How could it be done? On the one hand was my baffling experience with women and my deep opposition to the movement as such. On the other, the vast crowd of capable, intelligent women fighting to the death either for or against suffrage. I had no time to participate actively on either side. What little I did for the side opposed to suffrage brought forth such a swarm of condemning letters that my son Allan at least felt that every man's and woman's hand was raised against me. But after the little flurry I felt that my customers were nearly all sympathetic. Though I merely circularized them with a questionnaire issued by my side, the fact established me as a conservative among women and really added to my prestige.

I know many of the so-called grievances of women are false. No man ever unfairly discriminated against me. If one tried to, I, like everyone else, was equal to the emergency, and such experience really added a great deal to the zest of life. I felt that women, as a habit, overestimated their ability, and that they were too untrained even to appreciate the magnitude of their undertaking. I felt that there was already too much ignorance in government. I could see no good in increasing the illiterate, uneducated vote. Also I knew the hardship to little children when, by force of circumstance, their friend and mother was obliged to withdraw her companionship for the exhausting battle royal of politics or commerce. I had, perhaps, too high a sentimental feeling for woman per se, for — to me — the opportunity offered by life to women is far in excess of any offered to men. To be the inspiration is more than to be the tool. To create the world, a greater thing than to reform it. Also in my cynical mind I knew how potent was woman's influence over man, and questioned whether the vote could in any way increase that influence. But I was convinced that I must in some way utilize the great wave of feminine emotion. And then it was, and because of this thought, that the business of the obscure A. F. MacDougall burst forth into the glory of Alice Foote MacDougall.

A simple change. Much of the success of life depends upon keeping one's mind open to opportunity and seizing it when it comes. From the suffrage party I gained no direct advantage. One of their leaders, a noted society woman, wrote with quite amusing patronage that she would try ten pounds of coffee and, if it was good enough to suit her, would give me her trade. The ten pounds were delivered and the episode ended. When one is altering the face of the universe one cannot remember small helpful acts. But fortunately there were many kindly souls, men and women, who, not occupied by big reforms, could assist a woman struggling for another kind of independence, and with the establishment of my identity as a woman the business leaped forward to definite success.

In 1912, after five years at 129 Front Street, I was forced to move because the entire building was taken over by the sugar interests. Besides, my business was growing and I was delighted to feel that I could take the rooms offered me directly opposite, bright, sunny, and full of fresh air. Half my trouble seemed to fall from my shoulders as I established myself and my belongings in 138 Front Street.

Here, added to the sweet light of God's heaven came the sunlight of Allan's presence. A little relaxation came too, for Allan took much detail from my shoulders and relieved me of the strain of commercial traveling; and the growing business brought a sense of security.

At fourteen Allan, like his grandfather, had graduated with flying colors from Trinity School in New York. Then came the great question, college or business? Obviously he wanted to go to college, and undoubtedly he would have made a star football player. But I was thinking of what was best for him and for his future. Which was better, four years of semi-loafing or four years of learning in the college of business those things that would equip him to "carry on"? He had prepared for his examinations at Trinity School and presented himself at Columbia for his preliminaries. He passed with one or two conditions, but as he was only fourteen it seemed unwise to have him enter so young.

While I was debating, my mother died. During her illness I developed quite a serious sinus trouble, but of course had neither time nor inclination to have it cared for while she whom I loved so dearly was making the great transition. After it was all over my condition was serious, the cure was strenuous, and my work became an almost insuperable difficulty. So much so, that the thought came to me of what would happen to the children and the business if I should die. This thought was what really determined Allan's career, and having worked for two years in the Linen Thread Company, he came to me in 1913. His has been a triumphal progress. Always popular, he has inherited much of my father's charm and ability, and bids fair to make a good name for himself. Life unstintingly bestows upon him all its privileges.

He was sixteen when he came to me and our vivid experience together began. I had hoped to have him learn the coffee business in some office on the Street, but my ill health hastened his entrance into my business.

> Crabbed age and youth
> Cannot live together

was a little true in our case, and if I — and I did — send him off on business trips to catch my breath after a truly strenuous fortnight because of my partner's exuberance of spirit, he, I am sure, found a certain rest even when, to use his own expression, his errand was to sell coffee to a lot of "gabby old hens." (There were moments when Allan forgot the respect due his elders and betters.) From 1913 to 1915 were two years of happiness. Allan brought such joy into my life that it was easy to carry my burden.

A little event occurred at this time that indicates something of how near I was, for a brief time, to light-heartedness. Kelly, our expressman, was an ex-pugilist. Joseph, too, knew a good deal about fists. It occurred to me that these two might give Allan a few boxing lessons, and that it would be sport for him. He had not had time, of course, for much indulgence in sports.

On the evening of the first lesson I went home, for I don't enjoy physical encounters, and I did n't want my presence to dampen any fun Allan or Kelly or Joseph might get out of the fray. I did not see Allan until the next morning, and then he seemed glum, almost sour, on the subject of boxing. Evidently my frivolous idea of his getting a little sport had been all wrong. But I could get nothing from him in way of explanation. When I saw Kelly I asked him what had happened. "Why, nothing, Mrs. MacDougall," he said, "only he wanted to keep his eyes shut, so I just tapped him a little on the head." Before the end of the day I managed to get from Allan the admission that Kelly's little tap had knocked him almost senseless. His boxing lessons forthwith came to a sudden end. I told Kelly that I thought life would open his eyes fast enough.

After two years at 138 Front Street, the usual business cloud promptly arose. We were forced, like poor Jo, to "move on."

You see, men had been tolerant and a bit patronizing. I was not interfering with them. I was strictly minding my own business, so successfully in fact that gradually, instead of being small and unobtrusive, it began to take on quite offensive proportions. My purchases in the wholesale market were even being solicited. Those gentlemen who had n't wished to be bothered before now suggested the advantage of their stock, general service, and facilities. But in the dignified office building of 138 was rage and consternation! True, there were two elevators, but with them loaded all day with Mrs. MacDougall's incoming coffee, tea, and cocoa and outgoing freight, where were they, those lords of creation, to get up and down? They forced the landlord, and out I had to go.

Now, every move is a calamity in business. Changes of address almost always cause losses of orders and letters. New letterheads, billheads, advertising material, have to be printed and the actual cost of moving was an expense that caused me many a pang. You see I was still counting and saving every penny. Besides, another change had come. This was in 1917. The war had broken out and real estate in the lower section of the city had leaped into feverish activity. Every available office was occupied to answer the multiple demands of all nations, and those that were not occupied were being held at prohibitive prices.

Miles we walked, Allan and I, until unwillingly we were forced to lease the second floor of a building at 138 Pearl Street. Once a stately home in the early days of New York, afterward the offices of the Standard Oil Company, it had no conveniences of a commercial nature. No heat, no elevator, no janitor, nothing that answered to the needs of what was now a flourishing business with every indication of becoming more so. But there was no alternative, and here we established ourselves, and here I made one of those experiments that give zest to the game of life.

Everyone will remember the way prices soared as difficulties of transportation, shortage of men, and the immense consumption of the armies increased. As always, I was working with no capital, keeping myself desperately poor, running my home — as I have said — on a minus sign, and paying back into my business the most of my profit to take care of its ever increasing demands. This was quite all right, but not easy even in normal times. Santos, a low-priced coffee, cost about twelve dollars a bag at the beginning of the war. In two years it had risen to thirty dollars, and the high grades, Bogotas, Maracaibos, and so on, went up as high as forty or fifty, while Java and Mocha simply ceased to exist. The same was true of tea and cocoa. Men with large capital looked serious; for me it spelled ruin if I could not secure enough money to buy up a fair supply of coffee. Accommodation from my bank was hopeless. The president respected me, knew I was honest, yet nothing would justify a loan.

But one's brain is quickened by necessity. How adroitly it comes to our rescue in times of peril! I had gained by now the confidence of the people who bought from me. Long hours at night I lay awake thinking. Then I issued the following: —

SPECIAL NOTICE

Mrs. Alice Foote MacDougall regretfully announces that, because of conditions arising from the war, the following increased schedule of prices will become effective on and after May 10, 1916.

Coffee 2¢ per pound increase
(on all except fancy goods)

Tea 4¢ per pound increase
(on all except fancy goods)

Cocoa, 2¢ per pound increase

Orders received before the above date, accompanied by check or money order, *will be filled at present prices.*

It worked like magic. Eager to save themselves a few pennies in times when soaring prices made everyone poor, intelligent men and women seized the opportunity not only to save but to secure good coffee, when a little later it would have disappeared from the market. In a few days a snowstorm of checks came in with each mail, not only for immediate orders, but far in excess, for future deliveries. A crisis was passed. Unwittingly the public had financed me and my business. I could just squeeze through. Of course I kept faith with my customers. Their money was immediately converted into coffee, and as higher and higher prices obtained, they as well as I benefited.

This crisis was nothing compared to the new ones that arose because of the war. Events marched with rapid strides, taking one's breath away, leaving one devastated. Allan had become a member of Squadron A, a crack New York Cavalry organization, and with them went to Texas for six illuminating months of experience, a man among men. During his stay there two soft brown eyes smiled down upon him, and shortly after his return his engagement to Lorraine Allen occurred. Naturally, I lost my boy; but a wealth of lovely girlhood came into my life.

Then the darkness closed in upon me; the impenetrable war cloud enfolded me. In two brief weeks my sons and my brother Harry sailed to France to do their share in righting an atrocious wrong.   How I could have lived, had my sons not returned, I do not know, but even had they gone to return no more, as did my Harry, I could not have held them back, could but rejoice that they had gladly, gayly even, given themselves to their glorious duty.   Even so it was frightful, as every mother knows who had a son in the war.

And yet, strangely, life in one way was not quite so grim then.   A sympathetic feeling existed, born of common suffering and sorrow.   Everyone was in the same boat.   No one knew where or when death would carry off a loved one.   Life was stripped of its arrogance.   All men were brothers with a common purpose, the winning of the war. For once we were lifted out of artificiality.   We faced life bravely and truly as it is.

My boys' room was a dismal place after their departure, and at first I could not find courage to enter it.   It spoke volumes to me of their unspeakable danger, and, though bright and sunny, it seemed a hideous place of darkness without their presence.   But soon came the need for sleeping places for our men as they passed through New York, and the occupants became many and frequent.   I gave my boys' room to the boys of other mothers, and in doing so learned another lesson of faith in human nature.   At night my telephone would ring and a voice would say, "Mrs. MacDougall, I am one of the boys you met at the Navy Club.   I did n't know it was so hard to find a place to sleep in New York. You said I might call you up if I ever needed one. May I come now?"

How would you feel if you opened your door at midnight to a man you had never seen and let him enter and spend the entire night in the narrow confines of a small apartment? The war and the fineness it developed in men's souls helped, of course. None the less, it was quite an experience and most satisfying. Never once was my faith unjustified, my hospitality abused. After a little while, I had keys made which certain boys carried. That was a relief, for the irritating telephone bell ceased to waken me. The room was there. They came whenever they were in port. But it was sometimes a little startling when five extra men were there for breakfast. Many touching and appreciative letters came to me from them or their people. This one from a boy's mother pleased me :—

My DEAR Mrs. MacDougall, —

My son has again written me, of the delightful entertainment he has so greatly enjoyed at your home. I feel sure that being a mother with "two sons in the service, and a dear daughter," you will understand that from my heart I thank you for your kindness to my son, a stranger in a strange city. I wish it was so I could give any, or all of you, a small part of the pleasure you have given my dear son.

I can but think how many heartaches and anxious hours you must have had, with so many of your dear ones away in active service.

These are such awful times; the only hope one has is that this war may soon be over.

We hear such encouraging news from the other side, these days, that it begins to look brighter for our victory soon. I hope that all of your dear ones will return to you soon in health. What a happy time it will be when it is all over!

Very sincerely,
ANNA S. FOWLER

In those days I could not contribute to the War funds, but I became greatly interested in the War Camp Community work. Associating with me six or eight bright and attractive girls, I began giving parties on Sunday afternoons at my apartment. They began at three. Soldiers and sailors are taught to be prompt. As the clock struck, the doorbell would ring. I made a point of opening it myself, and sometimes my heart would fairly stand still as eight or ten men with evident embarrassment entered awkwardly, shyly. Three quarters of an hour of the hardest work I ever did would follow. Presently, however, under the influence of music, smiles, and cigarettes, the ice melted. Dancing began, and at four o'clock tea was served; at seven, supper. It was almost pitiful to watch the childlike enjoyment of these ungainly men and to contrast the happy peacefulness of those Sundays at home with the terrors that lay before them. Never shall I forget those great awkward boys and laughing bright-eyed girls playing "Going to Jerusalem" with the same zest they would use when firing a battery of machine guns. No, I shall never forget; for my chairs are a living reminder, not one unmarred. Some of them are entirely out of commission, some are merely not safe to sit on. All are veterans — and look it.

I shall never forget the great privilege of these experiences, or all they taught me of the goodness of human nature and the splendor of our young American manhood. This was my recreation after days of intensive work at the office. The heat, the work, the anxiety! I used to wonder at the courage of English and French women, when my own was taxed to the point of breaking in so very short a time.

Before Allan left, the business had grown so that we had an office force of fourteen besides ourselves. At the time of the "flu" in 1918 we were reduced to three, of which I was one, and orders were heavy. The whole force was reduced to Joseph, a little girl billing-clerk, and myself, and I sang again the old *Bab Ballads* refrain. Once again I went into the shipping room and weighed and ground, packed and shipped. Pride goeth before a fall. Only in my case pride fell before a saw and hammer and the necessity of making packing cases. The fact that I was no carpenter dawned upon me, and ever since I have walked with due humility.

Then, as autumn brought coolness and more endurable weather arrived, the "flu" came with it, and terror filled my heart lest the boy Joseph might go in a different way. Kelly, the faithful, cheery pugilist, died in two brief days of illness. What would happen to Joseph? But he survived, and with his return ended my days of humiliation and carpentering.

Then came one of those unnecessary sorrows that all but craze the mind. We were awaiting with impatience the arrival of another Allan, the third one, when a telegram came to me as I awoke one early Autumn morning: —

Regret to announce the death of Lieut. Allan Mac-Dougall in action September 17th.

(*signed*) THE RED CROSS

A scream escaped my lips, a sensation of suffocation, then brief oblivion. I revived quickly and set my teeth. Gladys, my daughter, never very strong, must be protected until there could be no further doubt of the truth of this awful message, and above all things Lorraine, the fair young wife, awaiting a little baby, must not know. Cables and telegrams flew to influential friends for verification, and a friend in the Red Cross in Paris corroborated the horrible statement. There seemed no doubt, yet I clung to one faint hope. Mistakes had been made; and the Government had not notified Allan's wife. Three weeks of torture unspeakable passed. Each day I wrote to him, my adored son, lest a silence on my part, were he alive, might cause him added discomfort. Every day I sat beside Lorraine and the little Allan, who came in the interval, and talked and planned for her husband's joyful return. She never knew my agony, never suspected my suspense.

Finally a letter arrived, dated several days after Allan's supposed death, and I knew he was safe still to bless my life with his radiance. Lorraine was well and the dear baby quite grown up before she knew of my great anxiety.

Harry's death followed quickly, and days passed in that distorted jumble of action and sorrow which comes with the death of a beloved one. The ordinary routine of business went on, while my soul agonized over the loss of this my first child in spirit, my adored brother.

As slowly the months went by, we knew the Hun was beaten, a fact he did not seem to realize. Then — who will ever forget the wild delight of the Armistice? First the glorious news flashing over wires and shouted through the streets. Then the heavenly pandemonium of bells and whistles. Forgetting all dignity, I rushed into the shipping room and flung my arms around Joseph's neck, kissed him, and shouted, "The war is over — the war is over, and my boys have not been killed!" No more business for that day. I tore up Wall Street, already carpeted with thousands of "scraps of paper." On the steps of the Treasury, and as far as eye could reach, men and women laughed, cried, and shouted. The pent-up anguish and anxiety of forty-eight months was let loose in tears of joy. Men, women, and children, old and young, rich and poor, joined in one great jubilation that war was over and peace had once more come. And our prayers were added to our rejoicings — prayers for those who had gone; for those who would not return. But more, more deep and earnest, that the horror might never be repeated.

Like all the other terrors of life, the war ended. I have always suffered so much pain that I had taught myself to prepare a kind of mental holding of my breath. When my back ached so that I did not dare to sit down, I consoled myself by thinking how divine would be the relief when the pain ceased. When anxiety made nightmares of my days and terror stalked in my room at night, I thought of the relief when pain ceased just after the birth of Gladys, and mentally holding my breath, I waited in the same way for relief to this other agony. Something of this philosophy helped me to endure that still more frightful pain — the war.

I had gradually accommodated myself to the discomforts of Pearl Street. An open fire in my office and gas radiators kept us at least from freezing. My chief anxiety was for the men who had to carry in and out, up and down those steep and narrow stairs, the heavy bags of coffee and the ungainly barrels of cocoa and chests of tea.

It is a dreadful sight to watch the stevedores

bending and straining under the terrific burden of unloading and loading the great ships on the water front. But far more terrible to watch the men I knew and cared for, carrying on their backs up those fearful, dimly lighted stairs, barrels of cocoa that weighed one hundred and eighty pounds and bags of coffee and chests of tea no less heavy. It was enough if they did it once a month. But it was all day, and every day; and since what had gone up must come down, after all these things had been hauled in in the morning, they were hauled out in the afternoon. A different appearance, maybe, but the same deadly weight. I could not watch them do it. I would run and hide in my private office, but I could hear their deep breathing and the heavy thumps of their feet. It told me all too plainly what they were doing. They knew how I worried, and smiled and bravely made light of it when I told them how sorry I was, how wicked I felt, and how surely I would alter conditions once the war permitted me.

The spring of 1919 my boys returned.

And now Allan was once more beside me. Donald went out on the road as a traveling salesman and brought in new customers every day. The business was really in a most flourishing condition. We were expecting it to increase still more and began leisurely search for more suitable quarters. We were in no hurry. Our lease had still about eight months to run.

Then a thunderbolt. That is the wearisome part of business — there is no peace, no sense of certain, permanent achievement, no stability. The unexpected, and usually the awful, is forever happening.

Upon opening a rather inoffensive-looking envelope one morning I found that the building had been sold and — would I move out at once, the new landlord blandly inquired, as wrecking was to begin immediately. Just like that — the building I occupied to be torn down, and not a vestige of another place in sight. Somewhat perturbed, I wrote to my new landlord, calling to his attention the fact that my lease had six or eight months to run. I said I would gladly vacate, provided I could find a suitable place. What compensation, however, would he offer me?

No reply. Only, in a few days, the building became infested with Italian laborers, and picks and shovels in their sturdy hands began the work of demolition. No words could ever adequately express the concentrated wrath I felt. As my rage mounted, so did my determination solidify. Ably seconded by Allan, I made up my mind: I would vacate when I was ready, and sooner or later this considerate landlord of mine would come to my terms and dance to my piping.

Days of utmost discomfort followed. One bitter morning icicles pendent from ceilings and rivulets flowing through the hallways proclaimed the fact that a water pipe had burst during the night.

I had always objected to the Elevated that roared and rumbled past our windows. But now it was nothing to the deafening crash of falling plaster and the sharp crack of breaking laths or of doors being torn from their hinges. It was a pandemonium, and one's nerves must be strong indeed to bear it. We brushed dust and chalk from our faces; clothes were covered continually by a fine coating of dirt. Callers were few in those days. A mild and unsuspecting reporter fled as from the trump of doom when a load of bricks and mortar casually came down the chimney near which he was seated.

And the heavenly joke was that my landlord had not done one thing to transgress the law. So far he had left me in the "peaceful enjoyment" of the leased premises. Technically, at least, for as a matter of fact my business was going on uninterruptedly.

And now it was a fight to the finish. In our few moments of leisure Allan and I searched high and low for a place to move to, and at last found, at 73 Front Street, one that would "do." That was the best that could be said of it. Four stark, bare, unplastered walls, divided into five rough floors with ladders in place of stairs connecting them — this was what we rented when Pearl Street would hold us no more. Alteration began to make it endurable, and the fact that there was a hoist, elderly and altogether disreputable though it was, consoled me, for now this wheezing, dilapidated thing would carry up and down my freight and no more would men strain and pant under the terrible burden.

Secure in the certainty of a place to go when our lease expired on Pearl Street, confident that sooner or later our landlord would be forced to come to terms, we sat down in what peace we could and awaited developments. Soon a letter arrived couched in much more friendly terms, and an agreement was reached: eighteen hundred dollars in cash, an enormous sum to me in those days. All moving expenses covered. We paid no rent for three months, which also eased the situation and somewhat reconciled me for my months of discomfort.

One can see the humor of an experience in retrospect. At the time it is a severe tax on nerves and physique and makes a salaried position attractive. But in creating a business one must needs meet just such ordeals and, conquering, move on to success.

This was 1920, the time of the Wall Street explosion. Wall Street has an atmosphere and a temperament of its own. I had felt it on many occasions. When the Knickerbocker Trust Company closed its doors in the panic of 1907, the air vibrated with anxiety and terror. In election years business there takes on a curious semi-delayed aspect, for men turn their whole energies to electing a president. Rather too frequently, I have always thought.

At noon the crowds are gay on Wall Street. Girls flash by in their smart costumes and young men relax for a few moments from the tension of office hours. On the day of the bomb, Wall Street was filled from curb to curb. Allan and I were on our way uptown to do some shopping in some precious minutes of leisure I had elected for myself. We were walking along William Street, noting the holiday aspect of the noontide throngs, when suddenly a curious screeching noise, a sound of tearing, rending, filled the air, and immediately in front of us a stream of glass flowed so fine in particles that it seemed fluid. Then a silence that was like an eternity, followed by the most hideous mortal sound, the cry of human souls in terror. No one knew what he was doing, what noise he was making, but human fear was vocal. The next instant there was pandemonium. Everyone rushed for safety, for cover, anywhere to flee from the terror of that spot. I can still see a boy dashing with big hops, his hair blowing, his arms trying to outrun his legs. He was multiplied by thousands. Human beings flowed like the plate glass of the windows in a liquid broken stream. We saw a poor little girl sitting on the curb, mute from shock, while a clerk picked glass from her hair and face as the blood ran down.

One minute I was thanking God that Allan was safe beside me. The next I was praying for the safety of Gladys, for I knew that my daughter had

had an errand at one of the banks only a door removed from the explosion. If she had followed her plans, she would be passing just at this time. I set out to find her. I was a mother hunting for her child, not a business woman. I was mute with agony until we could get back to the office, where we found that Gladys had escaped by five minutes that hideous spot of disaster.

Shortly after this, a new battle began for me at 73 Front Street, one of the most decisive of my life. Apparently larger opportunities were being offered to Allan, and they were tempting, for the men he had known in France were stepping into prominent lucrative positions, and he felt lost and submerged. But I had even at this time a certain intuition of large success. In it I wanted Allan to share. However, I could not still the fearful debate within me. Was my surety of success merely the trick of a mother's psychology, a mother who very much wanted her son to remain with her in business? Allan himself decided to stick it out with me. Of course to-day, seven years from that decision, it seems ridiculous that the question should ever have arisen. But at that hour success was just around the corner, and I was the only one who, apparently, had a sense of what was just beyond the bend.

When Allan had made his decision, the sun once more shone in our busy offices and I was glorified by the incorporation of the coffee business. In March

ALLAN MACDOUGALL

GLADYS MACDOUGALL

DONALD MACDOUGALL

1920, "Alice Foote MacDougall and Sons, Inc.," came into being with Allan as president and secretary, Donald vice president, and their mother chairman and treasurer. Grand and glorious names, as amusing as a child's regiment where everyone is an officer and there are no foot soldiers, but a joy to me after so many years of loneliness and struggle.

Success is an absurd, erratic thing. She arrives when one least expects her and after she has come may depart again almost because of a whim. Or perhaps the onward rush of her sweeping wings is stopped by a foolish, trifling obstacle. Our success came near being checked by a chimera, a fantasy.

Big corporations hesitated to buy our coffee because it was not roasted under the same roof with our packing and shipping departments and executive offices. This seemed a curious and unnecessary stumbling block. Just across the street it was roasted under perfectly adequate modern conditions. However, the opposition was insuperable. Eventually we had to load bag and baggage and move to 139 Front Street, where we have room to do our own roasting. From this turning point on, our progress has been rapid. The coffee end of our business amounts (1927) to about a million dollars gross annually.

Just one block north of that dismal room of my beginnings, the five-story building at 139 Front Street is occupied by our coffee business. The top floor contains a modern up-to-date roaster, working to capacity and producing six thousand pounds of roasted coffee every day. Below is a floor devoted to grinding, mixing, and packing bulk shipments. The third floor contains the canning. Yes, I said "canning"; for now we have to distribute through grocers, and no paper bag will stand the handling of the grocery trade. Small deliveries timed to suit the grocer's daily output prevent deterioration, and the hermetically sealed tin retains the flavor and freshness. Here too teas and cocoas are packaged and the smaller orders filled.

I have indicated something of the discomforts and inconveniences from which I suffered during the inception of my business. Nothing, however, was more trying than the lack of privacy. Always making physical comfort and convenience secondary, I worked, day in and day out, surrounded by my employees, deafened by the noise of the grinding machines, choked sometimes by the chaff of the coffee and the dust of tea and cocoa. No matter how intimate a conversation, each employee heard my most private affairs or witnessed my sorrow when death made me lose my self-control.

To-day the quiet of solitude is mine. My office shared with Allan only is a place of peace and quiet. I have a feeling of great attachment for that lower part of the city. Not only is it the scene of the battle I have fought with Fate, but it is invested with the atmosphere of purest romance

for me. Look at the ships lying idly beside the
quays, and visions of far-away lands, the tropics
and the Orient, rise before you. Walk along the
water front, and what paintings, instinct with life
and vitality, pass before your interested gaze.
Stand, and the flood tide of labor and its problems
overwhelms you.

On leaving the river, walk back, and all the
incidents of early New York life, the beginnings of
our great Endeavor, dawn on you. Barely three
hundred years since the first settler landed on
Manhattan, and now skyscrapers and the control-
ling power of the world where were the wigwam
and the Indian.

Coming still nearer in time are those days when
my grandfather did his "bit." What wonder then
that I should make of my office a little bit of early
New York? In it stands a nice old chair that
Grandpa Stephen used in the City Hall, and that in
those first dark days of my infancy cradled me.
For I was deposited on the seat — wide and roomy
— of Grandpa's chair while doctors, nurses, and
the whole family fought for my mother's life. I
sat in this chair when I signed a million-dollar
lease in 1927. But more of that later.

There too in my office is my father's desk, the
only one I have ever used since his death. There
is a lovely feeling of *closeness* when one uses some
article belonging to friends who have gone. And
here the uncovered rafters and the fireplace speak

of the primitive comfort of the early New York I love.

Just outside are the desks of our most responsible clerks and secretaries, and there is a little rest-room for my girls, where they can spend the noon hour and even cook a light meal if they wish on cold, stormy days.

On the ground floor, the switchboard facilitates communication with the coffee houses, private wires running to each one. And a busy board it is, for orders come in swift succession during the entire day. Here order clerks and salesmen congregate, and the coffees that are roasted in the morning — the day's orders of tea and cocoa as well — start on their journeys near and far, in obedience to the instructions of the occupants of this floor.

To-day my duties are varied and manifold. Each spring carries me to Italy to purchase new supplies for the restaurants and the ever increasing demands of our pottery and glassware business. This book has been written on the ocean, in Italy, and in France, and now as I write I am surrounded by the beautiful hills of New Hampshire.

Outside my window a golden sun is shining, the air is full of the song of birds, the farmers are gathering in a load of hay. It is such a June day as Lowell writes about. I am inundated with the peace that comes when, far from the cruel haunts of time-serving man, one is in the presence of God.

Twenty years ago, despair, illness, doubt, fear, and a something — a determination to win, perhaps. To-day, whether in the quiet little blue-and-gray office on Front Street, or here among the granite hills of New Hampshire, everywhere is for me a peace quite beyond the power of words to express.

IV

COFFEE HOUSES

FRONT STREET is only part of my story, and the
least spectacular at that.

In the very beginning I had realized the necessity of a more convenient location for marketing
coffee than Front Street afforded. But I chose the
district of lower Wall and Front streets, for here
is the centre of the coffee trade. Here the great
ships of the South and Central American trade
dock. Here are public roasters, here the generous
conveniences a great city makes for its enterprises.
Uptown one must seek post and express offices.
Downtown express wagons come to your door.
Then too there was a certain zest in invading this
very special district where men ruled supreme and
where the mighty pulse-beats of a world at work
could be distinctly felt. But if there were these
commercial conveniences, there were all but insurmountable obstacles. Women are not any too
energetic — at least as far as business goes. After
their business day, shopping, teas and dinners,
theatres and operas, the following morning finds
the telephone an easy solution to the marketing

question, and once one has the number it is far easier to add coffee to the grocer's list than make another call, or even to send a self-addressed postal.

This I found out all too soon, and it solidified my determination to have an uptown store. By 1919 I was spending between two and three thousand dollars a year in advertising, and I argued that this money spent in store rent would advertise the business, while yielding a return that could be measured in sales and good will.

For these reasons then, we — my sons and I — opened the Little Coffee Shop in the Grand Central Station, on December 9, 1919, and the first step was taken coffee-housewards. Small booths, twelve by sixteen feet, were being offered for lease. This was just as big a spot as we dared undertake. At first my idea was to use this tiny store only as a place to advertise and sell my coffee. One side was show window and door, giving on the corridor; the other three walls were blank, so I lined them with shelves to display my various grades and blends of coffee and, of course, the business step-children, tea and cocoa. We screened in a small part of the back of the shop, where we expected to store coffee on the premises, so that, as the shelves in front were emptied by a public voracious for good coffee, there should be no delay in meeting any sort of run on our stock.

That was a dream five years ahead of its time. For the hope that the coffee would sell fast, once we exposed the uptown public to it, proved fallacious. At the end of six months Allan wanted me to close the little shop, because it was almost a dead loss so far as dollars and cents were concerned. But I have a natural antagonism to giving up, once I have started anything. I simply don't believe in failure. In itself, it does n't exist. We create it. We make ourselves fail. Conditions present obstacles, of course, but there is a way to overcome them; so I hung on to our little booth in the Grand Central. Also I began to nurture it, as if it were a sick child. I had made the place look cheerful and sanitary, because any place connected with food must be clean and look clean, but now I began to make it a place of rest and beauty, a little haven to entice the weary commuter to sit down before the 5.41 leaves or he meets Mary Ann on the incoming 6.16. I made a point of being there on Wednesday afternoons to meet any friends who cared to come in. Sheer blue-silk curtains were hung in the window, and beside the packages of coffee and tea on the shelves I began to place brasses and blue-and-white china. Also I bought a huge electric percolator, and the delicious aroma of coffee filled the place.

The setting and the fragrance together began to turn the trick. Gradually people came in to buy their pound — or five, or ten — as they dashed for their trains, commuting for dear life. Sometimes they asked to taste my coffee, and before we knew

it we were serving coffee from tiny tables and all
unconsciously were laying the foundation of the
coffee houses.

Then, to my surprise, week-end guests began to
buy part of my atmosphere for presents — the
brasses and the blue-and-white china I was using
on the shelves to point up the simple color scheme.

I had long had a distinct fondness for the brightly
colored potteries of Italy and Rumania, and now I
tried to add these to my Grand Central shelves. It
was, of course, just after the end of the war, and
this pottery was almost unobtainable in New York.
Many a dreary ride on the Elevated downtown had
been enlivened for me by the sight of one window
filled with the gayly decorated plates and cups of
Rumania. Here I went first, and attempted to
order through this importer. He would sell me the
windowful of pottery which had cheered me so
many days, but that was all. He could fill no
orders. Having failed to receive the usual shipments from Rumania and Czechoslovakia, he had
written to his dealers there and had received this
reply: "Do not ask us to bake pottery. We have
no money to buy fuel to bake bread." He was
able to get Spanish pottery for me — for Spain had
not been crippled by the war — while I continued
my hunt over the city for importers who could
supply me steadily with Italian ware. Little by
little I managed to pick up here and there pieces of
old Russian brass and queer Chinese porcelains.

For you see I had found, to my great surprise, that I had two flourishing businesses: one, the sturdy coffee plant, the other, the flowering pottery. I was determined to supply my voluntary customers in the latter goods with what they wanted, though I pored over the classified telephone book by the hour in order to ferret out the importers who might possibly have stock. In a few months, however, I was able to import my first Italian china, through the kind assistance of my lifelong friend, Mrs. J. Walter Spalding.

This is the way to get along in business, I believe. Naturally one plans, organizes, and develops, but it is a wise woman who is also led, who is quick to feel the pulse-beat of her public and respond thereto. My business was coffee, but when I found the public wanted pottery, I let them have it. When I found that in a place like the Grand Central week-end guests wanted week-end presents, I purchased pretty little trifles in china and brass and copper to supply that demand.

This all happened quickly. It was just as though Fortune had decided to smile on us for a change; as though she said, "Now you 've worked hard. Here 's a sugarplum for your pains."

Then a new problem arose. The demand for coffee and tea was ever increasing, and it is an anomalous thing to serve a beverage alone. But what to serve with it? How prepare anything in that tiny shop? I felt that the limitation of space made the careful, immaculate preparation of sandwiches impossible, and I would n't have them unless they could compare with the coffee. Everything in life, you see, had to standardize itself to the excellence of the coffee.

This unsolved question was turning itself over and over in my mind, burrowing annoyingly deeper and deeper, when Chance, Fate, call it what you will, solved it for me and started a golden stream of money into my lap.

Do you know New York? Lovable as a dainty maiden in her Easter dress of smiles and flowers, adorable as a goddess abounding in plenty in her lavish distribution of presents at Christmas, she becomes a raging demon when the storms of winter assail her. There is nothing in the way of a storm that she does not indulge in, nothing that is possible that she leaves undone. After a day of gracious spring mildness, when the birds sing and one can fairly hear the young things in the ground waking from their winter sleep, the wind rises, swift, piercing, bitter. With it come squalls of rain, snow, sleet, and hail, in wearying succession and depressing fierceness. It is a time of exhaustion for the bravest, and one goes from place to place drenched and miserable.

Many such a day had I experienced, trudging wearily from place to place, delivering coffee or attending to the innumerable details of my growing business. This day on which "it happened" all was drear and dark and it was a courageous soul who dared go out except of sheer necessity. It was Wednesday, one of my "at home" days in the little shop. As I entered the Grand Central I found the huge corridors packed with a damp mass of miserable humanity. The air was heavy with that horrid odor of moist woollen garments, and a kind of steam filled each corner and hung gloomily from the ceiling. Under foot was a composite of mud, umbrella drippings, and sawdust. Pneumonia stalked up and down in fiendish glee, counting with ungodly mirth his many victims. It was a pitiful spectacle. I knew the symptoms. Many times had I been in just that condition.

On the impulse of the moment I telephoned my apartment, ordered my waffle iron and all the necessary ingredients, and placed a little sign in the window saying, "Waffles." A timid soul peered in. What did the sign mean? An explanation made good by a cup of piping hot coffee, filling the little place with its aromatic fragrance, and waffles, so delicate and crisp that they literally melted in one's mouth. Cream the richest, syrup the purest — an expression of contentment on the face of a man responding to the delight of good food, and lo! a million-dollar business was started.

When he offered to pay, I refused to accept any money. It was a joke, I said, a pleasure to do as I had not been done by in times when my need was great. For to-day, a pleasant episode to vary the

A CORNER OF THE "LITTLE COFFEE SHOP" IN THE GRAND CENTRAL TERMINAL

humdrum of everyday business, but never again; so why bother about a few pennies more or less? Thus I, who know so well the precious value of those same little coppers. But he and the rest who had crowded in said I must do it again. This was Wednesday, the seventh of February 1921. So rather reluctantly I said, "Well, just once again on Saturday"; and almost before we realized it we were serving coffee and waffles every day, and all day, and turning people away by carloads. A pleasant memory — a pleasanter surprise. We know about bread that is cast upon the waters. Who could think of such a return from a few waffles given away on a pitilessly cruel February day?

There is another side to my story that is not so spectacular perhaps, but far more lovely, it seems to me. The war was over, but the unmitigated horror of it was ever present in my mind. Somehow, I was impelled to create as much peace, beauty, and gentleness as I could, that there might be a tiny offset to the horror of that great iniquity. So I talked, laughed, and chatted informally with my customers. To my manager I spoke of gentleness and love, and little by little the pretty coffee shop took on an atmosphere of friendliness and peace. Often I worked late when every other place was closed to round out the day's sales, to add another pound or two to the sum total.

One Christmas Eve I was just about to go home. I was weary, and the inevitable sadness that creeps into one's heart on these festival occasions was my sole companion. The door of the shop opened and a timid, quiet, drab little woman crept in. The moment I saw her I knew she did not wish to buy anything, but we chatted together, handled over and over some of the pretty things I had for sale, indulging in the dull small talk of the shopkeeper. Finally, with a faint blush of shyness, she said, "Well, lady, I guess I'd better go now. You've been real kind to me." She hesitated, then: "You know it's lonesome in New York on Christmas Eve, and I thought mebbe if I waited round till the 11.20 for Waterbury went out, I might just see someone who seemed kinder familiar." I felt that the Little Coffee Shop had justified its existence, and that a lovely Christmas gift had come to me from Santa Claus. Don't you think so too?

Another day, one of steaming heat and humidity in mid-August, I was making waffles and a nervous woman hurried in, sat down, and ordered her lunch. My heart went out to her. I knew just the kind of vexatious day she was having. I knew her nerves were strained to the breaking point. Every bit of her suffering I knew. So I began to laugh and joke. Never did I cook waffles with greater care. And little by little I saw the pain pass and a look of greater repose come to her careworn face.

Months after she came to say good-bye. She was going back home. No more New York for her; but she said, "Mrs. MacDougall, this is the only place where in all New York I have found peace and rest." When people talk of success, I think of these two women and realize that I have had mine in full measure. Life does not offer many of us such rare opportunities to serve.

Another Christmas Eve I was again at my job, and a lady in deep mourning entered. She talked quite intimately of her sorrow, in that way that is often more possible to a total stranger than to one's relatives and friends. I think she gathered a little too of my necessity. After a while she went away. Standing behind the counter, I finished my last duties and then stepped out prepared to go home. On the floor before my startled eyes lay a crisp ten-dollar bill. Was it accident, or was it — as I like to think — a gift from one troubled soul to another? I do not know, but if her eyes ever rest on this page, may she accept my much-belated thanks. That Christmas the children had unexpectedly nice presents. For days Allan and Donald were quite insufferably arrogant, due to the blue of two new neckties apiece, and Gladys lost marks at school, because of her charming bracelet.

In August 1922 the crowds were so large, and the opportunity so obviously great, that a good angel appeared in the form of Mr. George Marshall Allen, a gentleman of ample means, my son's father-in-law. He loaned to us quite a large sum, and thus made our second coffee house in

Forty-third Street a possibility. It was a most generous act, a terrible risk for him, and a lifetime would not be long enough to tell the gratitude and responsibility I felt toward that kind gentleman. At present, I believe, he is contented, for his stock in the coffee houses is figured in six numerals. His purpose in lending us the money was that he wanted to see his son-in-law in a position commensurate with his own. To-day Allan is in a rather enviable position — head of three large and flourishing businesses, the father of two splendid little boys, with an adorable wife and a satisfactory position in the community in which he lives.

One of the most challenging experiences of my life attended the opening of the Forty-third Street shop, December 9, 1922. Our lease was most difficult. Our landlords — the Bar Building — were not altogether free agents, for they held a twenty-one-year lease from the august and mighty Bar Association of the City of New York, and many and varied were the limitations and requirements of that body. One of the lease clauses said that there should be no smell of cooking; and I, eager to secure this particular location, of peculiar and varied advantages, I who would rather die than do a dishonest thing, I who had for months cooked waffles in the Grand Central — I said they would not smell. And I honestly believed it. Imagine then my despair and consternation on

the day we opened! The air was blue outside
with smoke from the waffle irons, and it almost
seemed as if the odor of cooking batter could be
smelled a mile away. Added to this unexpected
horror, Sarah, the colored cook who had been with
me for years through thick and thin and unmoved
by either so far as she had ever shown it, Sarah
went to pieces. She was completely demoralized
by the amazing stream of customers, and began
to burn waffles with nervous persistency. Any
housekeeper knows very well what happened. I
set Sarah temporarily aside and myself generaled
the waffle irons. I had bought a new black satin
dress for the occasion of the opening, for I knew
people would want to talk with me as they did
at the Little Coffee Shop in the Grand Central. I
pictured myself "receiving," in a certain sense, at
this all-day tea-party we were inaugurating.

Well, my friends and customers did want to see
me; and they did see me, all smiles and batter,
my brand-new black satin dress showing the new
leopard-skin effect. I served as well as cooked
that day. There is a fire station near this location on Forty-third Street, and the firemen sent
in to ask if coffee and waffles could n't be sent in
to them. I took them in myself, poor Sarah by
this time being unable even to serve a waffle without dropping it.

But if Sarah was upset, what was I when that
day was over? My dilemma was not a passing

spasm of nerves. I stood face to face with one of the business crises of my life, and I knew it. Before opening we had figured out overhead and profits very carefully, and had anticipated daily about one hundred and twenty-five guests. Our doors opened at eleven and every seat — sixty-five in all — was taken. We closed at five with a first-day record of two hundred and fifty customers. A brilliant opportunity loomed before us. With ease a fortune was within our grasp. And all future glory and profit snuffed out in a cloud of waffle-iron smoke!

I never felt quite so discouraged in my life as I did that night. The place was empty. Everyone had gone home. Allan and I sat in the gloom and faced facts. Our landlords had every reason and every right to break our lease. Then what of our dreams, our hopes? Whence would come the rest I was beginning to want so very, very much? Once again eviction, but from a very different cause. And all the time the shame of my false — though innocent — statement to the landlord.

We are, of course, still occupying the premises. A ventilating system draws all odor and smoke up fifteen stories and it is dissipated in the air. It was not without travail that we hit upon this plan, but it worked, and that was all we or the landlord required of it.

And this very ventilating system gave me an

opportunity for an attractive decorative detail. When we opened Forty-third Street we had a pantry but no kitchen, for we intended to serve nothing but coffee and waffles, and these were cooked in front of people's eyes on tables made especially for the waffle irons. The ugly hood used to deflect steam and smoke from these tables was quickly turned into what we called a waffle house — a latticed, three-cornered-cabin affair under which a colored maid stood, suggesting the Southern-waffle, colored-mammy, log-cabin idea. Within a short time, however, we expanded our original plan of serving merely waffles and coffee, adding first sandwiches and then all the delicious foods we could think of. In March, four months after our opening, we served eight thousand people with three full meals a day, and by August 1923 we took on more space, doubling our seating capacity less than a year after opening.

It is hard to account for the unqualified satisfaction our coffee houses give the public. Our policies are simple: unerringly and unalterably, always the best the markets afford. I wrote to our various dealers telling them that we wanted the best, were willing to pay the full market price, and that if after this statement any inferior article was supplied, whether used or not, the whole amount would be deducted from their bill. This was a warning. On these terms and on these only would we place our business. The penalty has not been inflicted more than once or twice. We receive surprisingly uniform and satisfactory articles. Undoubtedly the quality of our food and our attractive service also contribute largely to our success.

In the early days of my struggle, when expenses had to be held down to their minimum and all luxury eliminated, I insisted that my own table should be attractive. There is an æsthetic side even to plain bread and butter. There is a spiritual significance connected with the gathering of the family for the common meal. Pitch food helter-skelter on a table, permit ugly, unlovely manners, and divorce a meal of all æsthetic beauty, and we approach the animal. But invest this function with something of the holiness of a sacrament by the addition of beauty and tenderness, and soul as well as body is uplifted.

So I assembled my maids before the opening of this new adventure, the coffee house of Forty-third Street, and spoke to them of the horror of war — whether in Europe or in our own souls, it made no difference. But if we each crushed ugliness and hatred and developed their opposites, if little by little the contagion of the beautiful spread, then ugly diseases of the soul, hatred, crime, and war would cease.

Applied to a coffee house, this meant the dainty service of the most simple dish, the careful, accurate preparation leading to this service, and the kindest, most thoughtful consideration of the needs and desires of our guests. Fortunately, I was speaking to colored women. There is in them a quality of gentleness and love which gave quick assent, and I was sure of their sympathetic understanding and fulfillment of my instructions; so perhaps our second avenue to success was built out of consideration and courtesy.

Waitress and hostess regard the people who come to our coffee houses as so many honored guests, and no effort is spared to make their visit, long or short, a time of peace and of repose.

But rest and peace are not, unless the eye as well as the body is re-created. Disorder in a room increases irritation or weariness. And even as irregularity and disorder create fatigue, so color used wisely is a beneficence; used unwisely, it borders on crime. Following this line of thought, I had decorated the Little Coffee Shop in the Grand Central Station in tones of soft brown, relieved by curtains of delicate blue silk, and had opened the new coffee house on Forty-third Street with the same restful and harmonious combination. Here also the walls were lined with shelves on which we displayed the quaint decorative potteries we were importing from Italy for this part of our growing business. I think that I must have felt what the Italian peasant feels when he satisfies his longing for color by painting brilliant hues on pottery, for the Italian landscape is softly toned. It is almost neutral in its many pastel shades, and when the peasant paints he picks out one or two or three of these and emphasizes them, using the full color against an ivory-toned background. It was this that I wanted to do in my coffee houses: against pleasing neutral backgrounds to display the pottery of the color-loving Italian.

Almost at once, a further use of this pottery developed. From the beginning I had retailed it from our shelves and had used it on our tables, for I could not imagine colorless china any more than I could white tablecloths in our restaurants. It makes food and drink taste better to be served from a beautiful plate and an interesting cup, and besides this, pottery amused and interested the guests. I had to buy it in quantity for our own service, so the thought of selling it wholesale was forced upon me. Within a short time I was buying each year in Europe many thousands of dollars' worth of pottery for our retail and wholesale business.

In the Grand Central I had learned that people were contented to eat with paper doilies under their plates, and to use paper napkins instead of laundered cotton or linen. Personally I have always abhorred the public napkin, because of the many times it is laundered. The use of prettily cut paper doilies and firm paper napkins had another virtue: it was economical. Against the dark walnut table tops, laid with paper doilies cut in imitation of Italian lace, the bright potteries of Italy were altogether suitable. To them I added colored glasses, here a violet one, here a green or a blue. At each place were set differently colored glasses and variously decorated pottery, but all blended into a bright, cheerful whole. It was a new note in the setting of the table, so of course I knew women would be interested, but men appeared to be too. I have had men tell me on leaving one of our coffee houses that they didn't know whether it was the food or the dishes that tasted so delicious.

My choice of varied plates may seem to have been haphazard, but there is generally method in my madness. I have always tried to supplement the color of the food with the color of the dish on which it is served. For example, just as white china drains the color from coffee, and an ivory-toned cup adds to its color, so a yellow-decorated plate goes beautifully with a green salad, especially if grapefruit tops the bouquet, so to speak.

Speaking of salads, reminds me of some of the fun I have had, playing games in business as I used to play in the Land of Let's Pretend. A good many people like a salad served with the main course, rather than separately. When all the dishes are round, there is a great deal of waste space, and the table looks awkward, too. So I availed myself of the crescent-shaped salad plate, so familiar in Italy and so unknown in America, that would fit half around the dinner plate. It was amusing to do, and it solved the salad problem for a good many men guests. Women seem more content than men to eat in the usual order of service.

One more detail, about cream and syrup. I had been annoyed so many times by skimpy quantities of thin cream served me in restaurants, and I was sure many other people had too, that I decided to serve not only the best cream and the purest syrup but a full pitcher of each, giving the guest a comfortable feeling of plenty. Very few people have ever abused this generous service. They use no more than if it were doled out to them in tiny individual pitchers, but they feel better about it. That's all.

The public is voracious. Once please it and, like Oliver Twist, it asks for more. After about eighteen months at Forty-third Street, our space was still inadequate. Again we must expand. Here arose an all but insurmountable difficulty, but the surmounting of it gave us our big opportunity, and, we believe, created a new idea in interior decorating.

One of my first axioms when I began business was "Don't do the stereotyped." People like variety. I always attempted to do and give the original. In Forty-third Street came my great opportunity.

The additional space available here was a narrow store thirteen feet wide, eighteen feet high, ninety feet deep. From it a stairway led to a huge mezzanine. The walls were sheer bleak spaces of white plaster, relieved only by the great ridges made by iron beams and girders. How reduce the height of this ceiling — how out of this narrow slit of ugliness create a thing of cosy warmth and restfulness? That was our problem. An oyster finding himself stuck with a grain of sand from which he must make a pearl is n't any more baffled than I was.

When one is working out a problem such as this, life becomes duality. One's ego transacts the ordinary routine of things, as if the mind had an upper and lower story and the regular perform-ance of the day's duties moved and motivated on the upper floor, while down below the all-absorb-ing problem toils silently, forcefully, toward its solution. At least this is how it seems to me.

From very earliest childhood my ears had been filled with descriptions of Italy, the most beautiful country in the world, and much of my subsequent reading had amplified the talk of my parents. At school, in art, literature, and poetry we were con-stantly taught of this same country and all it had done through its artists and poets to enrich the world with beauty.

So it was not strange that, in my perplexity, out of my subconsciousness should leap into concrete form all this beauty and that I should find it easily adaptable to our needs. I had traveled in Italy and one of the most beautiful remembrances I had was that of walls, broken and crumbling with age, and cracked by the strain of many storms and tempests; walls soft and beautiful in their dull greens, yellows, and blues; every crack filled with tiny vines or baby flowers, as if a kindly Providence, pitying the wall's grim resistance to the elements, had placed them there as a solace to their wounds. Those walls are a vision of paramount and unending beauty.

In the quiet of a sleepless night, there flashed upon my inward eye a vision of Italy, its irregular walls and doorways; its crooked, tumble-down stairs leading from street or courtyard, sometimes to the upstairs rooms of a farmhouse, sometimes to the loggia of a stately villa.

Then I set about applying my vision, realizing it in a modern fireproof office building. It was amazing how a hideously plain wall could be transformed. With a little chipping here and there, with coats of paint one after another of varied and different colors, the stubborn and ghostly white plaster yielded to my desires. Gay pottery and baskets and bright rags hanging on the always present clotheslines of Italy, quickly produced the desired atmosphere. In the Cortile, at 37 West Forty-third Street, you may find a little Italian courtyard — *cortile* — leading you gently away from the noises of New York City's sidewalks.

THE CORTILE

But really it is sometimes more than annoying, the way commonplace ordinary things stand in the way of your dreams.

Next to the walls, the stairs of Italy enthrall you. Almost always outside the house, they lift themselves in heavenly leisure and unevenness from the ground to the floor above. For many centuries men and women, barefooted or in sabots, have passed up and down, and gradually nice, comfortable, infinitely picturesque grooves have appeared. Of course I needed these grooves to complete the character of my stairs and add to the Italian feeling. But do you suppose I could have them? No. I tried it! People will step carelessly — though there were the grooves, if they would only use them properly — and slip and fall and hurt themselves. The next step is claim for damages, horrid words. After this had happened a time or two, all my beautiful authentic stairs had to be chiseled down again into a hateful, regular efficiency. The wings of my Pegasus were clipped.

During the excited days of the opening of the Cortile our second incorporation occurred and the Alice Foote MacDougall Coffee Houses, Inc., came into being with myself as president, Mr. George Marshall Allen as vice president, and Allan as treasurer, in March 1923.

The Cortile finished, we expected to fold our hands in sweet content and rest awhile from our labors. Vain and futile thought. The more we gave, the more insistent became the great good-natured public.

In spite of two additions the Cortile was soon all too small, and we knew we could profitably build another coffee house out of our earnings, if we had money in advance of those earnings. And so, mindful of Mr. George F. Baker's long-time kindness toward me, I went to him now voluntarily with a real business proposition. I asked him for thirty thousand dollars, to build a new coffee house, on the strength of the success of the present one on Forty-third Street.

He talked to me about the condition of the business, my plans, my prospects, and my policy, and asked for how long I would want the money. I said, "Mr. Baker, I want this money for one year at six per cent. I want it in three notes of ten thousand dollars each, with the privilege of paying it off at any time or interval in the interim." He gave me the money. I made my first loan in November. The new coffee house, the Piazzetta, opened on Christmas Eve following. In three months the loan, principal and interest, was paid off. I asked for a year. I paid in three months. I think nothing in all my life ever made me quite so happy and proud as that business transaction between myself and Mr. Baker.

And so, on December 29, 1923, we opened the Piazzetta at 20 West Forty-seventh Street.

Here I turned to Naples for the decorative
scheme.   Every city of Europe has its own peculiar
charm.   Naples of them all is the most simple
and direct.   It has no reserve; its trust in your
sympathy and understanding is complete.   It
takes you into its confidence and the whole performance of life passes gayly before your dreaming
eyes.   To most Americans the Bay and the hills
rising from it, a panorama of endless beauty and
wonderment, spell Naples.   For me it is the
streets and the street life that are enthralling.
The houses rise along the crooked twisting streets
in a multitude of colors, softened into sweet neutral
tints by the gentle ministrations of time and covered everywhere by lovely flowers, tons of them.
Who can wonder that the sunny Italian smiles
and is happy, bathed as he is in the warm lovely
air, gladdened by the always beautiful and ever
varying panorama, and enriched by the blessing
of countless lovely flowers?   And if by any chance
he is lacking these cheerful companions — lo, he
hangs out his clothesline and gay-colored garments take their place.   One gets to love the
clotheslines of Italy.

In the Piazzetta I tried to bring Naples to New
York.   There is always a little square — *piazzetta*
— in front of every cathedral in Italy, and this
shop became one by our turning the great glaring
forty-five-foot front window into the façade of a
cathedral.   Reinhardt's production of *The Miracle*

gave me my inspiration. The feeble architect whom I employed had been unable to think of any solution for the ugliness of this show window, but when I told him to build the façade of a cathedral with Gothic arches and a rose window, verily, he took me at my word and built two side by side. When you step through the doors of this façade, it is as though you stepped from an Old World cathedral into the customary piazzetta overhung with crumbling houses that are adorned with bright shutters, quaint little doorways, and balconies that wait for lovers. They do not wait long, for tables for two are tucked into spots as secluded as shutters and the illusion of romance can make them. Young New York has not been slow to search them out.

In the open court there are planted here and there the vines and bushes that all through Italy charm the eye and rest the jaded spirit of the traveler. And next to the flowers themselves are the gay and flowing clotheslines that fling to the breeze in a never-ending riot of color the peasant's well-washed garments. By such little touches, indicative of the very essence of the Italian landscape, we have made atmosphere. It has seemed to captivate the fancy of the public. Italy breathes her radiance about you as you eat, and colored maids moving swiftly, copper trays in hand, and wearing gay-colored peasant dresses with brighter contrasting caps, make an animated picture.

During the day sunlight and cast shadows lie on the crumbling houses that line the side of the Piazzetta. At night the place is flooded with moonlight, and flickering candles increase the animation and add their charm.

So far as I know, my idea to depict exteriors as the motif of interior decoration is entirely my own. Instead of trying to make our coffee houses look like drawing-rooms that had seen better days or boudoirs that ought not to be open to the public at all, I sought to make them suggest the easy, care-free outdoor drinking and eating places that obtain in Europe. To do this I did not attempt to reproduce the sidewalks of Paris, for example, where little tables line the *terrasse*. Rather I re-created in New York an Italian courtyard and a little square in front of a cathedral, where Americans could eat and drink if they wished. It has always been amazing to see how quickly they respond to the Italian love of ease and color.

Having once realized the delight of the public in this type of restaurant, events moved swiftly. For again in 1925 we opened another coffee house, Florence — *Firenze* — on Forty-sixth Street. Here again our interior was an outdoor scene from Italy. As space was more ample in this location, our imagination had wider sway. Now we were blessed with an able artist as well as architect, Mr. H. Drewry Baker, who made the elaborate work of building Firenze a pleasure, eliminating much of the exhaustion and irritation that less able architects had caused when we were creating the Cortile and the Piazzetta. Apparently there are architects and architects.

If you have never been to Florence, Firenze admits you to a taste of her charms. If you have been there, she consoles you for not remaining in that stately city of the Renaissance. Familiar sights greet you; the Ponte Vecchio, that famous bridge where Dante walked and Benvenuto Cellini lived; The Porcelino of the Mercata Nuova, beloved of all Italian children; the gracious stairway of the Bargello, and the very spirit of Italian street life haunts the tiny courtyard far in the rear.

Florence has a stately dignity and a culture of her own. Not one tittle has she changed since the days of Savonarola. True, tramcars and motors fill her streets, and tourists with their natural destructiveness do all they can to mar the loveliness of her old-time stateliness. But there she is, the goddess among cities, and one forgets the modern, the cheap, and the tawdry, and eagerly turns a corner sure of seeing a Medici, or hurries away lest a feud between some passing Guelph and Ghibelline shall break out. Gentle Romola sweeps sadly by and poor little Tessa lurks, furtively watching, at the trysting place, for Tito. On every side are places and sights made familiar by the poets and painters of the ages.

When we planned Firenze our problem was simplified by space, where building the other coffee houses had been complicated by lack of it. Here were a huge store and a large mezzanine. As I entered for the first time, the picture of the Ponte Vecchio flashed before me, and I determined to reproduce in hurly-burly New York as much of the charm of Florence as I could without her marvelous sky and a few other incomparable, priceless Old World things. I told my vision to Drewry Baker, and Firenze stands to-day as we planned it then.

As you enter Firenze, on your right the tall graceful pillars of the Mercato Nuova, a young thing of some five hundred summers, rise before you. For centuries this "new market" place has been the open-air scene of much chaffering and bargaining. One day it is baskets that are for sale; another, ceramics; another, Trina and Ricarmi, pottery, lace and embroidery in quick succession. And always, outside, the *porcelino*, that funny big boar, spouts water out of his mouth for thirsty little boys and girls.

In one detail of Firenze we have indulged in poetic license. For the beautiful old Ponte Vecchio crosses the store on the mezzanine, but without the Arno! With the best will in the world we cannot supply the river to flow under it. Instead, the public peacefully occupies tables and chairs where it should flow, and seems not altogether to object to the omission.

On the left, as you enter this coffee house, you see that part of the Arno known and raved over by painters for ages as the Left Bank. Here irregular houses stand out from the wall and are propped up by the rough logs of wood the Florentine has always felt sufficient support for them. Their soft yellows and browns blend with the green moss that covers all as with a veil, while a shutter is picked out from the mass of blended pastel by its splotch of bright green paint.

At the back of Firenze rises the famous stairway of the never-to-be forgotten Bargello. And here too, is one of the prettiest parts of all the coffee houses, a little Italian street. As you stand on the stairs and look down, you forget America and all that is therein, and for a time live and breathe the atmosphere of Italy.

In Firenze, as in the other coffee houses, sunlight, moonlight, and candlelight add their charm. Shakespeare says all the world loves a lover. I know I do, and hidden in quiet places are little tables where lovers or near lovers can enjoy themselves detached from the crowd, in the solitude they love so well. These places are never without occupants.

Apart from building the restaurants is the building of the organization, a duty carried most capably by my son. Little by little a very highly specialized body of men and women is being devel-

THE MARKET — FIRENZE

oped — a difficult job when one considers that there are about seven hundred employees (a contrast to the three of 1918) and that every day at least six thousand people are accommodated in our various places.

We like to do things well, my son and I, and we take not a little pride in this perfecting of our organization. Highly specialized women head each department, and calm and strong above them all is Miss Lillian Kennedy, our general manager. With patience and understanding she handles the multitude of problems a fast growing business like ours presents, and not only guides the women working under her but develops into strength those who in the beginning are weak, and educates and trains those who come without previous training.

To give pleasure to a few wretched souls; the knowledge that human nature craves the good things of life, in terms of nourishment, and needs beauty in form and color, as its companion; utilization of imagination and a long-suppressed love of the beautiful to conquer a difficult decorative problem; abiding faith that in all life two things alone are necessary, love and beauty, and that in business as well as elsewhere they are essential to a true success, and, adopted as a business principle will lead to success — these were the foundation stones on which this business, the result of twenty years of hard labor, was laid.

November 23, 1907, I went out from my little apartment a lone woman with a big fight ahead of me and dedicated to conquest.

February 7, 1922, I gave away a bowl of batter in terms of delicious waffles.

February 10, 1927, five years later, twenty years from my lonely beginning, I signed the lease for my fifth coffee house, — *Sevillia*, at 50 West Fifty-seventh Street, — the lease amounting to one million dollars.

In 1907 my rent was $240 a year.
In 1921 my rents were $4,650 a year.
In 1927 my rents were $169,175 a year.

To obtain this end, I sought and found, with ever ready, ever generous response, the love of my friends and the advice of several splendid men. Mr. Slee gave me freely and generously of his wisdom as a man who had made, by his own unaided efforts, a fortune out of "3-in-1" oil. Mr. J. Walter Spalding opened for me his treasure of wide experience as a merchant and financier. Mr. William H. Harris, a lawyer of wide experience, helped me with restraining wisdom when my impulsive nature would have run away with my judgment.

To my son I attribute my final success in this, my battle of life. From him also came my sunlight and my joy when life was full of sorrow and my footsteps faltered on the difficult path.

It is however to my three children, Gladys, Allan, and Donald, collectively, I owe my very being. In attempting to fulfill my duty to them as a mother, I met the challenge of their helplessness, their innocence, their dependence. Despising cowardice in others, I wished to prove myself no coward. Believing in the good, the gentle, the beautiful things of life, I addressed myself to the sweet duty of keeping these attributes for my children's sake and my own. And in striving to provide a living for them, I found a success beyond my wildest dreams.

V

ADVERTISING

"ADVERTISING is a disease, not a business." So said Mr. Spalding one morning as I sat talking with him.

Perhaps, but quite the most fascinating disease one can contract, the one department of a commercial enterprise that mitigates the dreary monotony of humdrum routine and admits of a certain hilarity in the day's work. Since it was to me a distinct and separate part of my business, I have segregated — so to speak — the account of it in this chapter.

From the very inception of my undertakings I spent money for advertising when I was not quite sure of having it for bread. The following embodies some of my reasons for so doing.

Competition *is*. In every business, no matter how small or how large, someone is just around the corner forever trying to steal your ideas and build his success out of your imagination, struggling after that which you have toiled endless years to secure, striving to outdo you in each and every way. If such a competitor would work as hard to originate as he does to copy, he would much more quickly gain success.

As I have said, the roasted-coffee business was almost unheard of at the time I was married in 1888. It is true, Arbuckle Brothers were wide distributors of the Ariosa coffee. But this was a harsh, crude, hard-drinking coffee, used largely in mining and lumber camps of the North and West.

Park & Tilford and Acker, Merrall & Condit carried the Java-and-Mocha, which was practically the only coffee used by people of social standing. Mr. Park and Mr. Acker of those two highly respectable firms came at regular intervals to Front Street. Though competitors, they always rode downtown together and, having purchased their aristocratic Java and spicy Mocha, returned to dispense it — two thirds and one third to the pound — to the waiting customers.

In 1907, however, almost every store on the face of the earth sold coffee. Grocers large and small, dairies and drug stores, department stores, many restaurants — hundreds of shops of all kinds and descriptions. Every friend I had seemed to have some relative in the coffee business. How was I, tiny atom that I was in the great seething commercial metropolis — how was I to overcome the resistance of the housekeeper to the new and untried, win her away from the established coffee of well-known repute, and distance this competition?

To undersell the market, of course, was my first device, but not an easy one when every penny was so vastly necessary to my small home and its occupants. Nevertheless, I sent out thirty-cent coffee under the trade name of #2 Special at twenty-eight cents, and the Java-and-Mocha that Park & Tilford sold at thirty-two cents I offered at thirty.

In those first years of my business I was a living example of the oft-repeated saying, "I drank like a fish." For I had to standardize my taste, and of course I could do this only by tasting. Slowly my palate was trained to the flavor of flat-bean Santos, of Peaberries, of Maracaibos old and new, Buchs, and Bogotas, and my eye at the same time was learning the differences in appearance of the green berries. Coffee as we test it on Front Street is quite a different drink from that made on the kitchen stove, and yet again different from that of the restaurant urn. Still again is it different with sugar, and when cream and sugar both are added, it may be called a delicious beverage but scarcely coffee.

So part of my daily dozen duties was to embrace each and every opportunity of drinking coffee. In homes and hospitals, in churches or at Childs', I drank what people served and fondly called coffee, enduring the unimaginable flavors of those varicolored and qualified liquids. Had coffee been the baneful drug some people claim it is, then surely must I have gone early to my grave.

Men of the coffee trade buy from standards and cup-quality. By this I mean coffee very finely ground, of which the weight of a penny — weighed on apothecaries' scales — is placed in a standardized cup. Freshly boiled water is poured on. After waiting till it cools and stirring thoroughly, one is able to get the real flavor of the coffee he is testing.

Gradually an idea, derived from the many flavors registered by my palate, grew of the kind of flavor I wanted, and my #2 Special was its product.

Then arose the problem of getting people to know and believe in me so they would buy from me. Here a serious difficulty confronted me, with which I struggled blindly in a way, and yet definitely, for years. There was antagonism to the woman in business, the blind antagonism of the skeptic, latent, unspoken, but consciously felt. Women would take the word of a dirty illiterate grocer who assured them that he carried the "best coffee," would pay him a high price, would drink a bitter unpalatable draught, and be happy. They would sniff suspiciously at the coffee I offered, would grudgingly buy a pound or two, and then return with contentment to the coffee redolent with mustiness of the corner store.

I was always conscious of this antagonism and struggled against it as I did against competition.

It is laughable now to hear the identical people extol our coffee as they buy it in twenty-five- and fifty-pound lots. Perhaps, too, letters of this kind helped, in which I emphasized my desire to help the housekeeper. The service note in my advertising was its distinctive feature. The following is only one of many possible samples.

Are you entirely contented with your present dealer?

Is his aim to make money for himself, or to protect *your* best interests? Does his quality always satisfy?

MINE DOES. Each and every cup of my coffee, when properly made, is fragrant, strong, and delicious.

Is his price reasonable?

MINE IS ON THE MARKET. Just the cost, plus overhead, plus a moderate profit. No middlemen, no commissions. I buy here at first hand and deliver to you direct. Does he pay carrying charges?

I Do, according to the quantity you order and the distance from New York. In other words, your coffee delivered in your home costs you no more than it does here in New York City.

If a mistake occurs in your shipment, does he rectify it freely, ungrudgingly?

I Do. Look at the guarantee on my postcards.

Place a trial order with me and know comfort in Coffee, Tea, and Cocoa.

Yours truly,
(*signed*) ALICE FOOTE MACDOUGALL

I rented a typewriter and began my advertising by personal letters to personal friends. I may say for truth's sake, in passing, that as far as appearance went, my letters were dreadful objects.

I am an impressionist by nature; I loathe detail; and I worked too fast on those letters for accuracy and relied on the good nature of other people to forgive my carelessness or make up with a little ingenuity my innumerable mistakes.

But my letters, bad as they were, carried my message, and I noted with joy and exultation that orders began to come in.

I used my own ingenuity and all my imagination to intrigue the public, to interest it, and to understand its needs and requirements. If you want the public to be pleased with you, you must be sure to please the public. The following letter, sent out, perceptibly helped in breaking down the resistance mentioned above.

A Home Keeping Experience of 20 years.

A Coffee Business Experience of 14 years.

THAT IS WHY you should let me select your Coffees and Teas for you.

I know what people like to drink at home.

I buy coffee green.

I know just how to blend it, just how to roast it, just how to ship it to you, so as to give you a more delicious drink at the price you want to pay than anyone else.

I do not view life or the coffee business from the grocer's viewpoint.

I have been a resident of New York City all my life and I know what New Yorkers like.

So I say that you should let me select your Coffees and Teas for you. I solicit a trial order.

If you do not like what I send, you can return it at my expense.

Knowledge of human nature is essential to success in advertising. I studied the whims as well as the necessities of the housekeeper and later of the various men and women whose business it is to supply food for larger places than the individual home, stewards of clubs, managers of hotels and sanitaria, and college fraternity houses.

If I studied the necessities of the housekeeper, no less did I study the attributes of my most recent offspring, coffee, so that I could give sound advice concerning its use.

Green coffee, like wine, improves with age. That is why my precious blue-paper samples were so valuable and costly. But roasted coffee deteriorates quite rapidly, especially when allowed to be contaminated by ill-smelling articles or subjected to dampness.

Among the many demons that beset me in those early days, none was more trying than the one who did not know how to make coffee the right way. So the following "Do's and Don'ts," printed on the gayest of colored paper, relieved my mind and made me laugh as I wrote it : —

Don't!

¶Don't start wrong and expect to make coffee right.
¶A dirty pot ought to make dirty coffee. It will. Even Emceedee can't prevent that.
¶Don't use a rusty tea kettle.
¶You can't see rust spots in coffee. You can't see appendicitis either.

¶Don't use stale water.

¶Even dead germs are not particularly healthful.

¶Don't use water that tastes of iron or lime.

¶While you require iron in your blood and lime in your bones, you should have absolutely pure, tasteless water for tasty Emceedee coffee.

¶Don't use last night's dregs.

¶The cup that clears off past regrets and future fears is made fresh every morning from good Emceedee coffee.

¶Don't get "coffee nerves."

¶In the first place coffee is a tonic. In the second place coffee is a food. In the third place there is n't such a thing as "coffee nerves" — if you use Emceedee.

¶Don't pay rake-offs, commissions, extra profits.

¶Emceedee is sold *to you* direct from the importer and manufacturer at the lowest possible price for which an absolutely A 1 coffee can be offered. I pay no commissions to your cook. I allow no corner grocer a rake-off. I sell you pure coffee, the best coffee, a full, heaping dollar's worth for each dollar — no more, but no less. Full quality, full measure, and a taste for your table that a king cannot surpass.

Do!

¶Do try Emceedee Coffee.

¶Just once.

¶In a new tin coffee pot.

¶New pot.

¶Grind one cup of Emceedee Coffee.

¶Fine.

¶But not too fine.

¶Then add water.

¶Just a little water to make a paste.

¶Put paste in pot.

¶Let water tap run 5 minutes.

¶Not 4¾ minutes — not 2 hours.
¶And good, real fresh water.
¶Four cups full.
¶In the pot, too.
¶Hot stove.
¶Twenty minutes.
¶Then ¼ cup cold water.
¶Right down the spout.
¶Stand 2 minutes — the coffee, not you.
¶Then serve.
¶And if you don't get the most delicious, taste-tantaliz-ing, sense-pleasing draught of nectar goodness, tell me — quick. Emceedee is the original-guaranteed-money-back-coffee.

The making of coffee is always a sore point. I tested and tried out the various ways and the utensils used in them. The result of these experiments led me to believe that there are three perfectly good ways of making coffee: first, the old-fashioned long-esteemed boiling process, which makes delicious coffee when done rightly, but is capable of infinite variations. When Mary the cook inadvertently leaves the grounds mixed with egg on the hottest part of the stove and omits the boiling water, lye, not coffee, results, and a husband's temper may be seriously incommoded for the entire day. If the egg is mere egg, not 3x or strictly fresh, wrath and abomination may ensue; so if you persist in boiling coffee (which of course should never be boiled), be careful. Of the other two ways, the percolator is all but foolproof, and this is why I advise it. Electrically made on your own table or by gas in the kitchen, you have only to follow the directions which come with the percolator to get a delicious result. The third, and of all ways the most artistic as well as satisfactory, is the glass filtrola. In five minutes you have a divine coffee if you use this method.

Next to experimenting with coffee the most important task was the making of promotion lists. They were made up from the Social Register first, then from telephone books, club lists, school lists taken spring and fall from magazine and newspaper advertisements. The selecting and compiling of all these was part of my daily work. My long subway rides were occupied by selecting names, my sleepless nights in cataloguing them.

You see I had to educate as well as to be educated, and a close study of conditions had to be made if the letters issued to the new lists were to be effective.

There was not much inward or outward sunshine in those days. My life took on a molelike aspect. Leaving my dark apartment early in the morning, I would burrow through the dismal subway and arrive at my sunless office to work through the mental fog of doubt and fear till night came; then the subway once more, dark, ill-smelling, and noisy, carried me to my home. One must have plenty of money if one wants sunlight in New York. Imagine then how grateful such letters as these were to my tired soul. With them came a burst of sunshine.

ALHAMBRA HOTEL, ALHAMBRA, CAL.
April 13, 1921

A far cry from B'way! Too far, alas! for a cup of coffee with you, since there has been no method of long-distance drinking as yet.

(If there were, think how convenient for the topers to keep their whiskey in Canada and drink it in New York.)

I wish you the very best, always.

Cordially,
E. V. B. POST

December 5, 1921

DEAR MADAM, —

This is to advise you that our Pomeranian pup, Sky-lark Chief Wa-Wa, will use no other breakfast coffee than your Mansion De Luxe.

Recently we ran out of your product and for two days were compelled to substitute another brand. The pup refused to drink the substitute, and inasmuch as we trust his judgment, which in this case corroborated our own, we immediately secured a new supply of Mansion De Luxe, whereupon the pup resumed his breakfast coffee drinking with every manifestation of delight.

Yours cordially,
GEORGE RANDOLPH CHESTER
LILLIAN CHESTER

There is romance in coffee. It comes from the ends of the earth, and goes to the far corners of man's habitation. Letters from all over the world come to me. For example, the following from China.

U.S.S. HURON, SHANGHAI, CHINA
April 18, '25

The enclosed check is to pay the accompanying bill.

Permit me to thank you for the regularity of your shipments and for the fine quality of coffee you have sent. Good coffee is not to be had out here, and yours has been mightily appreciated, not only by myself but also by my numerous guests.

I hope to resume my orders when I get established at home.
Yours truly,
VICTOR A. KIMBERLEY
Captain U. S. Navy

CORNELL HEIGHTS, ITHACA, N. Y.
Nov. 6, 1915

I enclose check for $4.80 for 20 lbs. of your Mansion Blend coffee, which is now established as our household coffee. The Bogota I use for especial occasions and it is universally smacked over by all who get it. I dare say you will receive occasional private orders.

Made properly, this grade has quite the rich delicious aroma and taste of the true Andean coffee we got on the spot, and I am not in the least disenchanted by the local setting.
Very truly yours,
LOUIS A. FUERTES

P.S. Drop a card to Mr. Frank M. Chapman, Amer. Museum of Nat. History, 77th. St. N.Y.C. He was our chief of expedition [to Chile and Peru] and might be much interested to know he can get the real coffee in New York.

I resorted to all kinds of expedients to save my letters from the doom that awaits so much good direct-by-mail advertising: the waste-paper basket. Sometimes letters went out in non-commercial envelopes addressed by hand. Sometimes I folded them wrong-side-out and placed a catch-penny or rather catch-eye phrase at the top to ensure their being read. Bills — as a mark of consideration — were sent to the man of the family, but letters were invariably addressed to women, for I believed that they had more leisure, more curiosity, and would therefore be more likely not to throw them away unread.

Believing that brevity is the soul of wit and that people are too hurried and impatient to bear with long-winded discourses, I went over my letters time and again, eliminating each unnecessary word and making as many arresting phrases as I could think of. At that time my business was all direct to the consumer, so

NO GROCER SELLS IT —
THE POSTMAN BRINGS IT

became a slogan that rang in people's ears so persistently that they ordered by mail to verify the statement if nothing more.

MORE JOY TO THE CUP —
MORE CUPS TO THE POUND

also had a convincing sound to the thrifty housekeeper's ears.

But I was not satisfied with results from letters. I needed more customers and the dangerous
envelope stood in the way of success. Besides,
letters were most expensive, costing at least
twenty-five cents apiece. This made me resort to
postal cards. The result was electric. A new
impetus had been given the business, and paved
the way for prompt response when the war
created dire necessity both for me and for the
customer.

The following card explained the "why" of the
rising coffee market.

Do You Understand Why Coffee Is So High?

Because the United States is about 1,000,000 bags short
of its usual supply.
Because Brazil is about 5,000,000 bags short.
Because of lack of ships to bring coffee to the United
States.
Because of high freight rates.
Because of starving Europe.

But — Do you also realize that

One egg costs (at least)	5¢
One pound of beef costs (at least)	45¢
One glass of soda water costs (at least)	15¢
One Cup of Mansion Coffee Costs	1¢

A Single Order — A Month's Supply

Ship by Express or Parcel Post, prepaid (in full or in part) according to distance:

	Per lb	
15 lbs. Mansion Coffee	42¢	$ 6.30☐
(an excellent coffee for general use)		
5 lbs. Bowling Green	52¢	2.60☐
(delicious for after dinner)		
3 lbs. Russian Tea (for family use)	56¢	1.68 ☐
1 lb. Ceylon Special (for the tea table)	80¢	.80☐
1 lb. Nutheart Cocoa	45¢	.45☐
		$11.83

1¢. a pound reduction on coffee when 50 pounds are ordered

Name_____   Address_____
City_____   State_____

A cross in the square.   A stamp in the corner.
Prices subject to change without notice.

(left margin, vertical:) ALL GOODS ARE RETURNABLE AT MY EXPENSE IF NOT WHOLLY SATISFACTORY

During the war my advertising ceased. Money was far too precious for saving lives to be spent this way. But it was essential to keep my customers informed of conditions and so I issued now and then market letters, thus keeping them in touch with me and the Street.

Advertising, to be effective, must be pursued relentlessly, and even then the results are so intangible that one's courage weakens. It was dreadful to see money flow out in this direction when I needed it so much in others. For a long time I really could feel little if any response. Looking back, however, I realize how that persistent reiteration of name and purpose gradually impressed the public. Possibly that public did not respond in terms of coffee purchases. Eventually, however, our crowded coffee houses were the indirect result. In fact it is fair to say that that small outlay of capital during fifteen years made advertising for them unnecessary.

But advertising does not consist in printed matter alone. All the small good-manners of everyday life, as well as the thoughtful consideration one shows for a friend's needs and peculiarities, may be practised to good account when building up goodwill, that best asset of a successful business.

As a child, I had been taught the use of the thank-you note and the bread-and-butter letter. This etiquette I applied to business. On receipt of an initial order, my customer received a letter expressing my appreciation of her patronage and introducing to her mind the thought of the other articles in my stock. Did she order coffee, in answering I also extolled my tea. If her household needed tea and not coffee, I tried to sell her cocoa as well, not alone as a beverage but as indispensable for cakes, pies, and frostings. I knew only too well the struggles of the housekeeper and the difficulties of the servant situation. Any labor-saving that I could suggest was sure to be a boon, so I emphasized the fact that my cocoa had all the richness and flavor of chocolate but dissolved easily and saved the necessity of being broken up and melted.

Bitter experience had taught me the appalling exertion of grinding coffee. One of my first purchases was a little grinding mill. Its hopper capacity was only half a pound and one valuable customer, the Hardware Club of New York City, used fifty pounds of ground coffee weekly. No matter how long I live or how old I grow, I shall never forget grinding that coffee. It took a hundred hopperfuls to fill that order, and I did it with my own good right arm.

To eliminate one vexation in the household, I taught my customers to buy ground coffee. Hard on me, but easy on the cook. Here again I had to educate, for there seems to be a funny superstition that coffee that is ground freshly must of necessity be fresh. So I advertised the fact that coffee leaving my office in the afternoon had been roasted that same morning; that my paper bags of lining, interlining, and covering excluded dampness and kept coffee fresh and uncontaminated, and that consequently a person could safely buy ground coffee, thereby producing quiet for early morning hours and the smile that won't come off on Bridget or Mary Ann.

I told people how to keep coffee after buying it, and I hope that future generations will rise up and call me blessed for this if nothing else. For I have taught many a person that clean and sanitary glass is the proper container and not the tin that mother used.

Plodding along day after day, utilizing every means that was fair and all the knowledge I had or could acquire, I relentlessly pursued, with inky tentacles sent through the mails, every man or woman who used coffee, tea, and cocoa.

I installed a card-catalogue system, at the suggestion of Mr. Slee, and soon I had a kind of composite photograph on each card. For each card represented all the needs and peculiarities of each and every customer, and customers are pernickety. One desires a light-bodied coffee which will not hurt her nerves, and uses the old-fashioned boiling process, so her coffee is Mansion Ground E. She buys five pounds at a time and wants five single packages. Her tea is Orange Pekoe with a dash of Oolong. She does n't want to be bothered to repeat these details, I know, so her requirements are jotted down, the last *t* is crossed, the last *i* dotted, and Madame merely telephones or writes, "Repeat my last order." A little trouble on my part, but one detail at least is eliminated from her busy life.

I arranged a set of composite photographs inside my brain. When I was writing a letter to the ladies of the Social Register, I pictured to myself all the idiosyncrasies, all the individual tastes and inclinations of the women on my calling list. I remembered that Mrs. A. knew, just *knew*, that coffee was poison. I knew that Mrs. B's husband smoked strong cigars and so killed his taste for delicate flavors. I knew that Mrs. C. suffered under the petty tyranny of a man who begrudged her every cent for the actual necessities, not to say luxuries, of life. I knew there were people of lavish expenditure, and I had to give them high-priced coffee or they would be discontented; others of limited incomes must be helped to a comforting delicious drink at a low cost. And when I wrote my advertising letters I planned their appeal to this composite person.

Another photograph stood before me as I wrote to that difficult, intelligent somebody, the *dietitian*. (Those individuals always think of themselves in italics.) Another, of the poor, poor harassed housekeepers of Chapter and on-and-off-campus Houses. That bewildered creature of many minds and oh! so little brain — the helpless shuttlecock beaten pitilessly to and fro on the Board of Governors' battledore. The crafty, self-seeking steward of the rich man's club was all but hopeless; but the woman of the telephone book, the commuter's wife with her well-trained, capable Main Street mind, was easy to convince.

Business becomes fascinating under this kind of psychoanalysis. Nothing helped me more than my pitiless method of cutting off from my soul the dead flesh of my self-esteem. Subjecting to

equally pitiless analysis the mental attitudes and
limitations of the public to whom I sold my coffee,
helped make a success of the coffee business.

Card catalogues are blessings and make a business healthy. But they have to be pruned and
fertilized as carefully as any garden or they become
an incredible opportunity for waste, full of information as dead as last year's weeds.

Not only must advertising educate, it must suggest. It is incredible, the slowness of the human
mind to absorb facts. We speak of seeing things
in the twinkling of an eye. Only an advertiser
realizes the fallacy of this remark. Blind are the
eyes of the most intelligent. After the Little
Coffee Shop in the Grand Central had been opened
five years, a lady came in one morning and said,
"How charming this place is! It's quite new,
is n't it?" I explained, and she said, quite
naïvely, "How strange! I pass here every single
day and this is the first time I have seen it."
After ten years, people who had received many of
my price lists were surprised to find that I sold tea.
Cocoa is still in the offing — but I have hopes.

One or two little flights into other fields of advertising proved the futility of the newspapers and
billboards for one located as I was, far out of the
way. I never pass a billboard without heaving a
sigh of remorse at the futile waste of good money
attendant upon my first, last, and only excursion
into that field.

But in all my advertising, as in all my life, I tried to practise the Golden Rule, foolish though it seems to say so. I did to others all those little acts of courtesy and consideration that are such invaluable helps in everyday life. I applied in my approach to others all the knowledge I had of life's difficulties and, with the limited means at my disposal, eliminated them as much as possible. I thought of myself and my own convenience not at all. In the beginning of my business I could refuse no order, no matter how small, and oftentimes went miles to deliver one small pound of coffee. The profit might barely be six cents, the carfare alone ten, but — you can never tell where lightning will strike. The man who bought only one pound a month might have a cousin who used fifty pounds a week.

Furthermore, when customers complained, I always assumed that I was wrong. Irate letters would come. "Why was the coffee I ordered under such-and-such a date not delivered?" We had never received the order. Maybe it had never been sent. Maybe it had been lost in the mail. Invariably I wrote apologizing and promising great exactitude in the future. Difficult discipline for a woman with a temper.

Did someone complain of the coffee being bad, a prompt apology was written, a new lot sent, and the old one accepted. It cost double labor, packaging, and expressage, but the customer was pleased and friendly relations were established. All of which was good advertising.

Sometimes amusing incidents occurred. A customer in Washington wrote saying that her coffee was quite impossible and would I please send some more and take this back. Of course I did, but I was really puzzled because I knew that in this particular instance the coffee was if anything unusually good. Great therefore was my relief when in a few days the lady wrote and amid profuse apologies explained that a new coffee-mill had caused the mischief, for, as the coffee was ground, so was the lacquer also.

Express companies are not always so careful as they might be. For example, if coffee is delivered in a truck with kerosene, it is ruined. It will even be affected if the truck has previously been used for gasoline or kerosene and splashed on the floor with either. The bag of coffee will be permeated with the odor.

My soul was wrung with anguish one morning when, on opening my mail, I read the complaint of a lady who claimed my coffee tasted of formaldehyde. Of course I told her to return the coffee she had, and a new invoice was sent to her. Then I set my mind at ease, for I learned that her husband was a doctor, and I did not doubt the formaldehyde was in her own storeroom.

There were however marvelously few complaints, rather many compliments. To make my letters more convincing, I printed a few of the favorable comments I received and all outgoing letters — I always tried to make a two-cent stamp do full advertising duty — carried these testimonials.

At present the coffee business has lost its original plan of selling to the consumer and has, under the able management of my son, greatly widened its scope. I smiled many years ago when Allan, aged fourteen, announced that he would "soon come into mother's business to inject into it a little of the masculine element." And, my word, but he has! Our advertising goes merrily on, now under the advice of Mr. W. I. Tracy, and I sit back — but I still do a few little things.

As I look back, however, the hours spent writing advertising letters and making dummies for postcards, seem high spots in a life of varied interests. In the times of deepest sorrow they brought a smile to my lips, and the response to them smoothed a path not any too easy.

VI

ACCIDENTS

COMMERCIALISM is the blemish on the fair face of American life. Fighting against the terrible conditions of the explorer and pioneer, our forefathers had little time to think of beauty. Hearts and heads became as hardened to the more gracious things of life as did their bodies against physical hardship. Little by little, as nature yielded before the dynamite of their wills, life began to express itself in the same hard terms, and the great commerce of a New World bent everything to its indomitable will. Adapting themselves to the size of the rivers, the mountains, the prairies, in short, the continent itself, our huge buildings are but monuments to the vision and power of our princes 'of prices. But to some of us the selfishness that is bred of great success is our shame. We have subdued the wilderness and made it ours. We have conquered the earth and the richness thereof. We have indelibly stamped upon its face the seal of our dominating will. Now, unlike Alexander sighing for more worlds to conquer, we should address ourselves to adding beauty to that glory and grandeur. That people are eager for and appreciative of beauty, the success of the coffee houses proves; nor would the story of their conception be complete were not due emphasis given to this side of the business.

Americans ignore the rules of life. Sleep may be reduced to a minimum, food to a daily ration eaten hurriedly, when and where is most convenient, and most of the laws of nature may be set aside when we have a thing to do and want to do it. But after a while tired Nature asserts herself in no debatable accents and demands relaxation.

This was what happened to me when my first-born coffee house, the Cortile, was about a month old. Old pains returned. I walked with difficulty, stooping, and that most trying of conditions, brain-fag, made me speak hesitantly. I constantly forgot the word I wanted, and was unable to express myself freely, even when irritated — and then at least I usually do not lack power of expression.

I was tired out. Money was not very plentiful. We had gambled our all on Forty-third Street. I faced the possibility of losing all I had spent in labor and initiative during fifteen long, weary years if the Cortile failed. Signing the lease for that store was the thing that took courage. My million-dollar lease caused me not a qualm. I had then already gambled and won.

When at last the Forty-third Street place was running smoothly, I went to Allan and stated the facts. I told him of my physical exhaustion, and that I feared a mental breakdown. I said, "I'll take a new gamble now, a thousand dollars on a trip to Europe against an insane asylum." You see I had worked for fifteen years without a vacation. My day's work was rarely less than fifteen and for a long time eighteen hours a day. I really was very tired.

So one eventful day I departed. During all my early life I had filled my mind with dreams of the Old World. As I write this chapter now at Nice, the Mediterranean stretches wide in all its beauty before me and the dreams of those girlhood days are realized as I hear the lap of its gentle waters. But twenty years ago, as the prison closed its doors and my sentence began, I had banished my dreams, and all hope of seeing that land, which was so familiar to me in book and picture, was put aside.

When I sailed in the spring of 1923 I was too ill to have much emotion. A long voyage lay before me. In a sense I was as insecure of the future as was Columbus, for my broken health bereft me of ordinary initiative and to face the unknown land of Italy, its currency and speech, seemed an ordeal. I felt no interest in my arrival. I had been swallowed by an immense fatigue. All I wanted was rest — oblivion. But with the first immortal crack of my *cocchiere's* whip, the first delightful bray of the donkey I encountered on the pier of

Naples, interest revived, and soon the beauty of Italy and of the gentle laughing Italian people overflowed my senses and life began anew. It inundated my soul — this beauty — as some great river its banks, and revived in it all the love of form and color that had been buried for years under piles of little brown coffee berries and dried-up dusty leaves of tea.

Hard and cruel seemed the commercialism of my own dear land. I longed to have some of the Italian "know how to live" added to our "know how to get."

After my return, refreshed in body and in soul by beauty and gentleness, I spoke to my staff and to my servants of the ideal I had found in Italy and brought home with me. Added to the routine performance of each day's work there must be the ingratiating smile, the sympathetic understanding that would make our coffee houses places of rest for New York, as Italy had been a soul-reviving experience for me. The gracious "*buon' giorno*," the gentle "*buona sera*" of the poorest peasant, and of each and every clerk and shopkeeper abroad was a benediction to ears accustomed, as mine were, to the irritable discourtesy of commercial America. But not until sometime later did .the idea of utilizing the characteristic features of the Italian city occur to me. How it happened has already been told, but the interesting and inexplicable fact is that that enforced visit to Europe by one seeking

MRS. MACDOUGALL, HER DAUGHTER, HER SONS, AND STAFF
MANAGERS ON THE DECK OF THE S.S. CONTE ROSSO

rest should have borne fruit that paid so well in developing a purely commercial enterprise.

It is one of the mysteries of life, the way the casual proves to be the important. I have learned to feel that it is an essential of success to be very sensitive and adroit in knowing how to turn these accidental happenings to one's own advantage.

What is success? How does it come? What causes produce it? In writing of my life, the answer to these questions may be of interest to women and I will at least attempt to indicate some of the causes that I feel have contributed to my success.

Many times during the years of what I must feel was an eventful life, some simple and ordinary occurrence has thus led to results of wide importance for me and for my business. For many years I evolved my own advertising ideas, wrote my own copy, attended to my own printing. Guided in the beginning by Mr. J. Noah H. Slee, I carried on alone until I reached a point where I felt in need of a brain more capable and trained than my own. I felt that my methods, as well as I, had gone stale. Opportunely one day, as I sat at my desk, in October 1921, Mr. Harry A. Stewart, a gentleman who was beginning to make his mark in the magazine world, called to see me. I had known Mr. Stewart because of an interview he had previously given me for an article for the New York *Evening Post* and the memory was a pleasant one. Mr. Stewart was

a little shy, a little retiring, but some chord was
struck between us and a sympathetic understanding was established.   I was glad to have it renewed
and listened with interest to his plan for publicity.
As a result, I met Mr. Stewart once a week.

Our opening story set the pace. "Sex is
woman's best business weapon." I remember
shrinking a little before Mr. Stewart's quizzical
nonchalance. But his judgment was justified.
The story went like wildfire and was quoted
throughout the entire country. Magazine articles
followed. It does not pay to be squeamish in
publicity.

For at least two years I went every week to Mr.
Stewart's office in the Metropolitan Tower, twenty-
eight stories above the humming, seething world
below. He would say, after the usual greeting,
"Give me five good reasons why a woman should
not go into business"; or, "Tell me whether college is essential to the business woman." Then
would follow a discussion of perhaps an hour.
Sometimes the humor of some ridiculous proposition would dawn upon us, and jokes and laughter
formed a pleasant interlude. Sometimes I came
to him depressed, and his understanding soothed
and comforted me. Finally that story was produced which was "good copy." But whatever we
said was literally gobbled up by the papers.

It was great fun as well as great publicity. It
was an accident that led to big results, for finally

an article in the *American Magazine* told my story
to an audience of two million readers.

The newspaper stories always began: "Mrs.
Alice Foote MacDougall, left with thirty-eight
dollars and three children" — How tired I did get
of that woman and those interminable three! But
the stories filled other people with interest and
curiosity and the coffee houses filled up in consequence. How like some bearded lady or dog-faced
boy of the circus, I sometimes feel as the public
asks to "look at me."

After a short and markedly brilliant career as
a writer, Mr. Stewart passed, the victim of war
injuries received in France.

Another casual occurrence led to the most successful of advertising campaigns.

Life is beset by many annoyances, and those that
stand out above all are the life-insurance and advertising agents. The latter especially raise my
wrath. For, with urbane smile and perfect seren-
ity the advertising man takes your precious time
to explain in detail how you may separate yourself
from thousands or millions of dollars according
to your reputed wealth. He spreads before your
bewildered eyes layouts of one kind or another, and
calculates with nicety what it will cost you per
second, minute, and hour for a longer or shorter
period. Then, pleased with his eloquence, he sits
back and smiles, a benignant angel, at your diminishing bank account. And you — you say, timidly

paraphrasing Little Peterkin: "But what good will come of it at last? What will I get back, and when, and how?" Then the gentleman becomes vague; prophecy is not his *métier*. "One never can really tell, but the chances —" and so forth and so on.

Having been accustomed to this kind of thing, I read, in February 1924, with half-hearted interest, a letter from Mr. W. I. Tracy. His business was advertising. He had a plan for me, and it happened that I was just at that moment in a somewhat receptive mood. As before, I felt the need for a new and better-trained mind. I felt that the time was ripe and the money ready for an advertising campaign.

You see, my business is coffee, and I love it. Imagine my astonishment then, to find myself the head of a restaurant business! To be sure, the restaurants were the living advertisements of the coffee business, but at this time it was a case of the tail wagging the dog, and poor little Front Street was quite lost to sight under the nimbus of the Cortile, the Piazzetta, and Firenze. So I wrote Mr. Tracy. I rehearsed my various experiences with his predecessors and said I had thought I was finished as far as advertising men were concerned, but if he could propose a plan whereby instead of spending all the money I had or ever hoped to have, I would stand a reasonable chance of a fair return, I would gladly listen to him.

In the course of a few days I had my first personal interview. I was delighted. Here was a
man of charming personality who knew his business, just as Mr. Stewart knew his. He had vision
enough to understand my viewpoint and my advertising needs. He convinced me of his ability.
As I sailed for Europe again in the spring of 1924 I
left to him and to Allan the details of the campaign.
Thanks to Mr. Tracy, our outlay was small, our
success amazing.

But perhaps the most fantastic of these accidents
came through my own Donald and the Plattsburg
training camp during that period before our
entrance into the World War, when Theodore
Roosevelt and Leonard Wood were trying to arouse
a pacifist professor of a college town into active
duty as President of the United States.

Toward the end of camp, in 1916, I received a
letter from Donald saying he had met "a peach of
a boy," and could he bring him home when he came.

Enter Drewry, at that time an attractive boy of
sixteen, cultivated and intelligent. He is now the
architect of the coffee houses. I had floundered
around first with an architect who knew so much I
could never reach his highly turned-up nose, much
less his understanding, to tell him what I wanted,
though he heard me quite distinctly when I spoke
in terms of cash. Then I had struggled with his
successor, who was as dull and limited as anyone
could be. After these two it was joy to associate

myself with this bright, intelligent, beauty-loving young man who, at twenty-five, having graduated from Princeton, was now an associate in the office of Carrère and Hastings. In building the Cortile and the Piazzetta, I battled with stupidity and ignorance. I had draftsmen — that was all. When we created Firenze I had that most delightful of all contacts, a soul that stimulated mine, an ability that was equal to every occasion.

Quite by accident also came Frederic Sanseverro, an Italian who does all the color work in the coffee houses. What fun it is to stand beside him and watch the uncouth white plaster of an office building turn into the many-colored, many-creviced wall of an Italian inn, or to see the girder that supports the ceiling change from soft plaster into worm-eaten old wood. All by the deft use of chisel and paint brush.

And what greater joy than to stand back and watch the activity of these three young men of the coming generation, who have contributed so largely to the success people so kindly attribute to me. Allan, thirty-four, clever, adroit, resourceful, grappling with apparent ease the intricate problems of heating, ventilating, electricity, or the terms that shall constitute a favorable lease for us.

Drewry, twenty-seven, a man tingling with beauty and transcribing on blue prints a maze of intricate detail and exquisite workmanship, the vision of his soul.

Still again, Sanseverro, adding color, and with color radiance and life, to the whole.

The humble waffle should not be without its due recognition in this chronicle of accidents. In a way it was the crowning accident of all, for it pointed the way to our coffee houses.

It has been cumulative and progressive, this endeavor of a woman to care for her children, but the progress has been punctuated by just such fortuitous experiences as these. Hence there comes a feeling of a Power who is a "very present help in time of trouble," and a great humility and thankfulness abide in one's heart.

The burden is heavy, the sorrow cruel, the trial long, but always the trail is blazed with the help of understanding friends. Great minds send their inspiring philosophy like beacons on one's way and here and there the unexpected happens, and at the right moment assistance comes, and deliverance follows.

The day that I signed my million-dollar lease for the new coffee house on Fifty-seventh Street was one of great commotion on Front Street. Many orders kept the roasters busy on the top floor, and below the various machines for grinding, milling, blending, mixing, and packing were working over-time. In the offices, the faces of my busy girls were flushed and their excited fingers made the keys dance to a lively tune. Newspapers telephoned for this interview or that, the photographers, reporters, lawyers, notaries, and the principals and owners arrived to assist a woman in signing a million-dollar lease. It seemed to be something of an event to these others, and I too felt a thrill. But to me it had a deeper significance, for was it not the *release* from my life sentence of twenty years at hard labor?

As I started for home that night, Joseph stood before me, cap in hand, a generous smile lighting up the features of the face I loved so well. "Well," said he, "Mrs. MacDougall, I have been with you twelve years. I know what you have been through. I am glad you have succeeded, and I'm glad to be a little part of your business." Dear Joseph! Do you realize all your faithfulness has done to bring about such success? Joseph came to me as a boy of sixteen and we worked shoulder to shoulder on those first days when big orders taxed my small office force to the point of breaking. I taught him to wrap up our parcel-post packages so that the wildest attempts of postal employees would not break them open, and on dreadful days when orders requiring special grinding or special packing overwhelmed us, I ground and packed with him.

In the chaotic times of the war, never did he hesitate. When express companies failed, when all kinds of impossible conditions arose, Joseph always did the impossible — strong, smiling, willing,

THE PATIO — SEVILLIA

MRS. MACDOUGALL'S NEW COFFEE HOUSE

faithful. One rule dominates us: "All orders must invariably be delivered or shipped on the day of their receipt." Knowing the dilemma of the housekeeper when groceries do not arrive on time, I had made this rule at the very outset of my business. It is as forceful to-day as then. And to this rule, in spirit as well as letter, Joseph was *semper fidelis*. It is pleasant to feel that as the business has developed so has he, for now he is manager of the roasting and shipping departments of our firm.

Arriving later in the organization, as entry and bill clerk, Agnes Hunter has now become an expert accountant, the head of all the intricate bookkeeping the two corporations require. Every detail is on her finger tips; no minutest item escapes her vigilant accuracy. Of a frail, supersensitive nature, not any too strong, blessed or cursed as it may be with a New England conscience, she works early and late with untiring zeal. The immediate world of Alice Foote MacDougall would cease to revolve if anything should ever happen to Joseph Meyer or Agnes Hunter.

And the same devotion to the best interest of the business seems to inspire each and every one of our employees. Why? Because it is their business, and we, the owner, and they, the employees, work together for a common end.

All through these long years of business experience, I have tried to keep the human side uppermost. A "soulless corporation" is a horrid-sounding phrase; for what is life, whether in the human body or in a big corporation, without the constant daily inspiration of the soul? It has always been a meaningless phrase to me, for never have I found a soulless thing in all my journey through life. But if there were such a thing, I conceived it to be part of my business to keep it very far from being in any way connected with my endeavor.

I have felt it a privilege to suffer, since it has made my understanding more complete. And I have earnestly endeavored to add sympathy to my understanding and to keep myself attentive to the wants and necessities of my employees. As a result I have their confidence. I am not "I." They are not "they." We work together, and the success of the business is "ours."

I do not have much time to read, and therefore make the following statement with the conviction borne of observation only. To me the Labor Party has committed its greatest crime in belittling the dignity of work, in dragging it down to a poor thing of hours and pay envelopes, and of killing in the workers the fine sense of pride in a job well done, no matter how lowly. There was a time when the laborer loved his work. As he beat out the pattern on some exquisite piece of silver or carved the consecration of his soul into some piece of old, well-seasoned wood, he received from himself to himself a payment in joy beyond the power of money to buy. What machinery has done in depriving him of opportunity, Labor has done far more cruelly in making him the pitiful tool of the time clock and pay envelope.

A little of the joy in work well done remains, and still goes on. In the kitchens and dining rooms of the coffee houses, as well as in the offices, and the roasting and packing rooms on Front Street, emphasis is laid upon the artistry of each and every man's and woman's work. Accuracy of detail, beauty of the finished product, whether a well-made package of tea, a beautiful cake, or a leg of mutton perfectly roasted, everywhere we try to inspire our employees with the feeling that "the joy of work is work's reward." A one-sided programme, you say. Quite so. We ask perfection of labor and we try to make each man's salary commensurate to his ability and to his needs. But we do more. We want our people to be happy, and we reason that only can they be so if their work is beautifully accomplished. Since, however, our exactions are heavy, since we ask free and willing service of our employees, and an accuracy and perfection far in excess of others, so we feel obligated to recognize the service they give us. Consequently a bonus is given to each and every employee according to length of service and perfection of work.

Our bonus meeting is a joyful affair. Once a

year, just before Christmas, our employees assemble and then my sons and I give to each man and woman the bonus earned. When people speak of the atmosphere of the coffee houses, of the feeling of restfulness and peace as well as beauty that one finds therein, I hope that it emanates from our kitchens and service rooms, where contented and interested employees work for the benefit of our customers.

Work brings success. Long hours, conscientious plugging, an open mind to opportunity, and a ready adaptability contribute to it. Merchandising is easy, a simple process of arithmetic and a clear sense of a just relation between outgo and income. But success is a dull and cruel thing if we stop here. Really to succeed, we must give ; of our souls to the soulless, of our love to the lonely, of our intelligence to the dull. Business is quite as much a process of giving as it is of getting.

VII

MY PHILOSOPHY OF WORK AND RICHES

ONCE there was a man who had lost his way in the high mountain passes of Switzerland. It was cold and the shadows of night were closing in upon him. Just then a little peasant boy appeared and the stranger asked of him, "My boy, can you tell me where is Kandersteck?" And the boy replied, "I do not know where Kandersteck is, sir, but yonder lies the road."

In the same spirit I have written this book. I do not know the way to the Kandersteck of success, but certain paths lead there, and that woman is rich indeed who follows them.

I constantly receive letters asking me how I have achieved this thing that men call success. What have I done to produce it? What has it done to me? Apparently the world is full of poor women who are left with children and no means of support. They are careful readers of magazine articles and having read a so-called story of my life, want me to give them the Open Sesame prescription.

I cannot do it. No one's problems can be solved

by another. Conditions and the qualities of souls differ too much. To me life means the growing of a soul. I do not know why this duty is imposed upon us. I merely know that it is, and I feel that we are given much latitude of free will. We do not know where Kandersteck is, but the way lies clear before us, and the soul has qualities that may be developed for guidance on our way. And so we proceed. From the poor little bewildered embryonic thing of small ideas and limited vision, through torment and despair, until at last the richness of life and the glory of its great opportunities dawn upon us and we are at rest.

I feel that I have lived deeply, vividly, and that, if my life has any meaning to those outside of me, a little of my readjustment may be interesting. I wish I could write better, that I might explain it better.

In the beginning was wild rebellion, complete loss of faith. If anyone could have been brought up with less equipment than I, I do not know her. One idea was firmly fixed in my mind, that the world was made for my enjoyment and everything in it must adjust itself to my pleasure. My religion had a good deal of the reward-and-punishment idea about it. It was principally luxury I expected, for my sins were not glaring. That is to say, my virtues and my sins were about the same as the rest of the people among whom I lived. I thought of myself as did one of our colored servants. Walking into her kitchen one day, mamma said, "Lewis, your kitchen is a disgrace. Everything in it is higgledy-piggledy, everything is untidy, Lewis, and I am afraid you are dirty." Six feet of dark-skinned complacency stood first on one foot, then on the other, and nonchalantly toyed with a greasy carving knife held between more greasy fingers. "No ma'am, Mrs. Foote, ma'am, I is n't dirty; I 's average." Average, my sins and my virtues. For the rest, the world then as now was a pleasant place, peopled with friends full of unmitigated kindness, consideration, and helpfulness.

When the change began, I was totally un-equipped to meet it. My revolt was complete. Why did God single me out for such punishment? What had I done to deserve it? Others not one bit worse than I were living in the lap of comfort and contentment, while my soul was torn by bewilderment, grief, and despair. I was, in the accepted way, good. Why should I be singled out for such dreadful punishment?

From this attitude of mind began the long, slow process that gradually led to a new philosophy of life and to an understanding of the divine purpose in all things that makes life supremely sweet. Now, instead of the old futile debates and ques-tioning, is security. In place of doubt, is assur-ance. Contentment has superseded fear.

Because of the success business life has brought

me, even because of this very philosophy of peace which I acknowledge has been achieved through overcoming the obstacles business offered me, many people wonder why I still advise women not to go into business. Perhaps those who read this book may get a clearer vision of what the price of business is to a woman.

But if one must pay this price, if Fate leaves a woman no choice in the matter, if she is to fulfill her duty, if it happens that life ordains her for work instead of leisure, then let her go to it. She should forget individuality, traditions, inheritances, strip for the game as does the athlete, relieving her soul of all unnecessary impedimenta, and then address her enterprising spirit to the free and careless enjoyment of the great adventure. Business for women is inevitable in many cases. When it is — then make it a fight to the finish and get a great deal of satisfaction from the fighting. Pay a big price, and pay it cheerfully. I am conscious of the sniff of derision that my mid-Victorian attitude must arouse.

To the college girl brimming with the enthusiasms of her youth and the rather false information given by her worthy professors — persons whose knowledge and vision rarely go beyond the college campus — commercial life means emancipation from endless tiresome details of home life. Especially if she has been reared on a farm, visions of the exhausting, soul-destroying cares of the farmer's wife must lend powerful support to the professors' talk, and the glamour of office life in a big city shines alluring and resplendent to her innocent eyes.

Business life to the efficient salaried individual presents less terrors, surely, than to the woman who attempts to blaze her own trail. To the salaried clerk, no matter how low or how high her position, life is comparatively easy if her budget is accurate. So much to send home to parents or to help a sister or brother through college; so much for possible ill-health; so much for board, lodging, clothes, charity; so much, if possible, set aside for old age. And the overplus of pleasure a big city gives freely to everyone alert to atmosphere and beauty produces a quite comfortable condition for soul and body.

But it is to the woman who departs upon her own adventure and attempts to create, who pays rather than receives salaries, who is not to be satisfied by running in a groove but must initiate, it is to her I say — Don't!

The terrible uncertainty. The silence and aloofness life takes on when one is in the midst of the hand-to-hand fight. It is the lack of understanding in well-meaning friends, it is struggle and poverty, it is loneliness and despair, that constitute the salient, integral parts of the thing men call business. If a woman thinks the battle worth while, let her go to it. My advice is — Don't.

What, then, must woman do to win in the world of business, once she has entered it? What qualities must she cultivate, what characteristics suppress, what others develop?

First of all, it seems to me, she should honestly inventory her abilities and limitations. So very many of us, in business or out, overestimate our abilities. When I was growing up, Bill Tweed covered New York City with the shame of his iniquity, and I can still quite distinctly hear my mother say, "If I were mayor of New York City, I'd soon put an end to Tweed and his gang." How many of us say the same sort of thing, and believe it, until the event proves its impossibility. The suffrage party was equally sure of this ability to purge politics, yet the changes they promised have not materialized. Not because they are not sincere and earnest, but just quite simply because they don't and did not know what they were undertaking.

This overconfidence in one's own ability is the root of much evil. Vanity, egoism, is the deadliest of all characteristics. This vanity, combined with extreme ignorance of conditions the knowledge of which is the very A B C of business and of life, produces more shipwrecks and heartaches than any other part of our mental make-up.

Honestly take into account your inability. Don't camouflage yourself. See yourself as others see you — or at least try to. Don't imagine you are Napoleon when you have n't even the qualities of his valet. If you are sure of the weak points in your character, if you are quite conversant with your limitations, the best corner stone of success is laid. Do not arrogate to yourself qualities that you have not; but for heaven's sake don't forget that of all God's creatures you have the highest opportunity, and that your sphere is limited by the heavens only.

So, if a woman enters commercial life, let her inventory most carefully her limitations, and build herself up where she finds herself lacking.

Again, if she is to win she must suppress all traditions that are likely to limit the free flight of her spirit. This was the very hardest thing for me, I think. I had never seen my mother wash a dish or do any sort of manual labor even about her own home. Ladies did n't do it at that time. And it took a great deal of spiritual development before I could look on myself and my fate rightly, because I had not only to wash dishes but do all sorts of work for other people, sewing, mending, anything that brought in a few pennies, in those years before I made the plunge into an actual business office.

One must eliminate the traditional and cling to the essential.

Then there is always the question of health to be considered. Many women think themselves delicate when they are really only lazy. Half of the so-called ill health is imagination or nerves or both.

The other half has for component parts indolence and the joy of wearing a martyr's crown.

Life is not precious, a thing to be cherished. The soul and the mind are the instruments God gives us for our use and half of us don't begin to use them. We put Life and Health on two little pedestals and spend most of our time performing acts of devotion before them. Instead of using them as a carpenter his tools, as a helmsman the rudder, to hammer or steer our way to victory, we turn ourselves into Vestal Virgins with nothing on the face of the earth to do but to feed the feeble flames of our comfort. Life is no craven thing, lurking coward-like in a corner. It is big, broad, splendid in opportunity. It is to be used, not cherished. It is to be spent, not saved.

Faultless honesty is a *sine qua non* of business life. Not alone the honesty according to the moral code and the Bible. When I speak of honesty I refer to the small, hidden, evasive meannesses of our natures. I speak of the honesty of ourselves to ourselves. In the still watches of the night, have it out with your soul. Honestly size up your smallness and cultivate bigness of outlook, of charity, of understanding, and of sympathy.

Imagination is a valuable asset in business and she has a sister, Understanding, who also serves. Together they make a splendid team and business problems dissolve and the impossible is accomplished by their ministrations.

And what a luxury of riches follows in the path of our imagination! Give it free wing and it solves many a problem, creates the conditions that hasten success. Imagination concerning the world's wants and the individual's needs should be the Alpha and Omega of self-education.

I think a large portion of success is derived from flexibility. It is all very well to have principles, rules of behavior concerning right and wrong. But it is quite as essential to know when to forget as when to use them. Your rules are yours and they may be as relentless as you please for yourself, but don't carry them farther than that. You are not your brother's keeper, and even if you were your rules would probably not apply to his needs and behavior. Much less in business must you adhere to the rules set up by yourself. I had a coffee business, but flexibility added a pottery business and practising the Golden Rule led to our large and flourishing restaurants. In business you get what you want by giving other people what they want.

A necessity always makes a better business — or at least a more dependable one — than a luxury. I selected coffee as my business not only because it was a sheer necessity, but because, through my observance of affairs, I feared a business that dealt in luxuries.

I had a passionate love of books, and in the early days of my marriage I had the privilege of frequenting the bookshops of Mr. Alphonse Duprat, a bibliophile of wide learning and great discrimination. But I learned a lesson from him which I applied in after years. When times were good and money easy, when Wall Street smiled, Mr. Duprat could easily sell his priceless Elzevirs or some lovely Book of Hours once cherished by the haughty Mary of Scotland. (I still remember when I held that book in my hands and felt the thrill of touching what she had touched even while she plotted the murder of Darnley or Rizzio.) But in bad times his business withered like a flower during a drought. My necessity was too great to tamper with so sporadic a thing. Coffee was necessary — more so perhaps in bad times than in good, but always a comforting and delicious drink. So coffee was my choice. But in the beginning friends offered many and varied opportunities based upon the get-rich-quick idea. To each and all I said No, with thanks. I knew I had chosen a hard, slow road, but I also knew it would pay in the end. It was merely a question of push, perseverance, and prayer.

In all the wide gamut of human experience, nothing plays so important a part as faith.

Faith — not the poor little thing recited in five minutes at church on Sunday morning. Faith that is as broad as the heavens and as wide as the earth. Faith that comprehends in its vast sympathies everything human as well as divine, and carries one with the swift sure wings of the angels directly to his goal.

But my faith did not confine itself to the things of religion alone. Perhaps nothing in all my business has helped me more than faith in my fellow man. From the very first I felt confident that I could trust the great, friendly public. So I told it quite simply what I thought, what I felt, what I was trying to do. And the response was quick, sure, and immediate. Trust is a great thing. In fact, all constructive thought is powerful. It is the small doubts of timid souls that accomplish their ruin. It is the narrow vision, the fear and trembling hesitation, that constitute defeat.

Have faith in God. Trust your fellow man. Believe in yourself. And life becomes a triumphant advance, and one approaches death itself as the last great adventure in that unfinished episode men call life. "God helps those who help themselves." There were times when I wished God had n't given me quite so much latitude in this respect, but it was necessary for my development. To faith in God add faith in man, add faith in one's self.

But it is a lonely programme. The very virtues you cultivate become walls that inevitably separate you from your kind. Life takes on a new glory, it is true. Fear falls away, vanquished. Contentment and peace reign where once were rebellion and despair. A new danger comes to your soul, and intolerance and impatience with those who are as you have been all but destroy that which you have taken such pains to build up. Not alone are there spiritual barriers between you and the friends that you have, but your business training has made your mind incisive. In the swift rush of business you have no time for small debates and petty dilemmas. You have not time to think even of possible failure. You depart upon an intended action or policy. If you succeed, all well and good. If you fail — well, it simply means double time till you catch up. Often you put in eighteen hours of work because there is no one with whom you can play. Work thus becomes at once a delight and a tyrant. For even when the time comes and you can relax, you hardly know how. And those who can relax with you are too far away, energizing their own sphere with the wealth of their intellects, or — like you — have forgotten how to let go.

Age also plays its part. One may look young and feel young, but at forty a woman has only a little of the girl's resiliency. Men, unhampered by the physical limitations that women endure, can play all night and still work all day, though even men cannot go on forever. But the woman has to have more rest, to build up tissues broken down by the wear and tear of being a woman. After a day of hard work, it is not always possible to recreate oneself at concert or theatre. We go home and go to bed.

And our homes. Those lonely bachelor-maid affairs! An attractive apartment, the phantom of a real home, a bird or dog or cat in place of children. The questionable companionship of near marriage, in some cases. In others, books and periodicals as a substitute for one's husband's brain and companionship.

All this, every step of the way, takes courage and is exhausting. We all know courage in its accepted terms. To me the big courageous acts of life are those one never hears of and only suspects from having been through like experience. It takes real courage to do battle in the unspectacular task. We always listen for the applause of our co-workers. He is courageous who plods on, unlettered and unknown.

The boy awaiting his captain's summons, the soldier listening for the call of zero hour, the man on the Stock Exchange watching the ticker fluctuating to a panicky market, or you in your own home at the bedside of your little child, feeling the pulse beat of his fluttering heart — all, all need courage. Courage not alone in the free-for-all of the business day but in those still, silent hours of the night. In the last analysis it is this courage, developing between man and his limitations, that brings success.

One should have a mental house-cleaning before going into business, for many well-established ideas are erroneous. Among these is our attitude toward poverty.

Poverty is relative. If you want a Rolls-Royce

and are forced to ride on the tram, provided you allow it to disturb you, you are as miserable as the man who is starving to death in a cellar or dying of thirst on a raft at sea. Poverty is the result of bad adjustment between the soul and its desires. We pity the poor. Yes, they are always with us and to be pitied. But don't forget — they are also to be envied. Think of the joy of not needing a bathtub, of not being dependent upon soap and water! The person who has been accustomed to these, suffers when forced to do without. In the days of great poverty, I did not mind the sensation of hunger. A glass of water is inexpensive and quite a satisfying lunch. But, as I have already said, to be deprived of tooth paste, to brush the teeth without it, was a dreadful thing, a daily discomfort.

It was a real struggle to give up my subscriptions to current magazines. I have a peculiar possessive quality in my love of books, and hated those I got at circulating libraries. I wanted my own, clean and personal to me. I wanted the joy of marking passages that pleased me, to which I could refer at some future time. And there were many weeks when even the public libraries were impossible for me because of lack of time. For leisure is essential in selecting the book you want, and I had no leisure. This for me was one of the trials of poverty.

One experience is common to the always poor and the newly poor alike, the lack of privacy. One would never go to a man of wealth and ask searching questions as to his expenditures or the amount of his income. Yet no more embarrassing and discouraging thing ever happened to me than the self-constituted right of relatives and friends to first-hand knowledge of my most private affairs. How much money did I have? How much rent did I pay? Why did I buy this for my children? Why did I send them to private schools? I had no money; there were the public schools, giving a good education (Heaven save the mark!). What right had I to send them anywhere else?

At one time a worthy but not overintelligent relative sent me a hundred dollars as a fund for my children's education. I had a beautiful time calculating what I would do with the income of this princely sum, invested and drawing six per cent per annum.

People were forever telling me to live within my income. Gladly, provided I could find it. How people love high-sounding, well-known, and familiar phrases! No advice could have been more futile. My income was a matter of pennies seized when and where I could. I was always in debt, and payments on account here and there gave us the necessities of life. Once the rent was paid, I prayed for money for the next month. Having allayed the fear of the butcher, I smiled down the suspicions of the milkman till pennies enough accumulated to reassure him in a more practical way. I could tell my outgo. My income was an unknown quantity, except as the books of the business showed a definite profit on each pound of coffee.

I do not mean that people were purposely unkind nor that they were especially curious. They sincerely wanted to help me. But the incessant questioning racked my soul. Introspection and self-questioning as to the sincerity of my motives increased till I was brought to the verge of despair. Forced one day to ask a relation, a rich man, for temporary assistance, partly to help but far more to please his self-esteem he went over my wretched books with a magnifying glass. Why did I keep a servant? Twenty dollars a month — how hard had he worked as a boy to earn twenty dollars! *He* knew the value of money. At the outset of *his* life he had never allowed himself such luxury; why should I? I asked him to tell me how I could be in my office working and at the same time cook, dust, make beds, and look after little children. "Well — well, well," he hesitated. He had not thought of that; and he passed on. Three hours' grilling and I left. Less chance than ever for sleep that night.

Poverty is relative, and lack of food and of the necessities of life is not necessarily a hardship. Spiritual and social ostracism, the invasion of your privacy, are what constitute the pain of poverty. Added to the constant attempt to keep my personal life my own, a thing that kept me always on the defensive, I was unable to be part of the society to which I had been reared. It was only one more straw, but it added its burden to my overladen back. I had no time for society, no energy, no vivacity for it.

I have spoken of the servant I kept. Perhaps no humiliation of poverty is more trying than that inflicted by one's servant. People of this class are so often the veriest snobs, ignorant and yet sophisticated. Full of a knowledge born of the frightful intimacy of domestic service, they are devoid of feeling or charity. Their wages are their gods, and once you lapse, you stand convicted before them, a being worthy only of contempt.

I employ many servants now, principally colored. Among them is Saidie, whose story shows as well as anyone else's one of the frailties to which flesh is heir.

Years ago Saidie came to me. After three or four days she gave me notice. I was very anxious to keep her, for she was an excellent old-time servant. But she explained that she could not stay. "You see," she said, "I am accustomed to living where one can go over every piece of furniture with a fine lace handkerchief without soiling it." I stood convicted, I who loved cleanness and hated dirt and disorder; but I was working at the business for dear life and a period of two or three weeks before Saidie came had reduced the apartment to

great untidiness. Each morning a few hours of
intensive cleaning, dusting, and sweeping I had
done, to be sure, but my limited strength had little
effect upon the dirt of New York, so Saidie, sniffing
superciliously, departed. A few years ago this
same Saidie appeared at one of our coffee houses
and was employed. Not long after I was amused
to hear her boasting of the fact that at one time
she was "the madam's" household servant. She
is still with us, contented and happy.

In fact our servants all seem happy, but just back
of them I often see the sinister face of my colored
maid in those dark days, years ago. I knew I was
supporting my home, three children, and that maid,
but how many more because of her depredations
I could only guess. During the long days of my
absence at business, with the children at school,
what use did she not make of my apartment?
What cooking, washing, and preserving did she not
do in my kitchen, using all the gas she needed and
whatever supplies she could steal? And I was
almost glad to have her do so, provided only she
would stay and relieve my weary ill-health of the
strain of cooking and cleaning. Yet, with what
self-righteousness and lips curling with scorn would
she show her contempt if her wages were not paid
on the tick of the clock. Gossiping with my
tradespeople, she knew just how long they waited
for their bills and, knowing better than I how much
of those selfsame bills could be laid to her stealing,

still would show by her contempt how much she despised me for paying so slowly.

Of course I could buy no clothes for myself in those days and kind friends gave me clothes they no longer needed. So in spring I received winter clothes, in the autumn and winter the thin things of summer. I sweltered in summer in a winter dress and for years never knew what it was to be warm in winter. I shall never forget the acute agony of my fingers in winter as I went about delivering coffee. How the string cut through my thin, shabby gloves.

But hunger and cold, ill-health and pain are nothing. They pass. The thing that remains is ignorant criticism, well-meaning but futile advice, the contempt of a subordinate, the feelings of the under dog. The amazement he feels at the kind of people who kick him. The despair at his helpless inability to resist. Always duality. The life of the under dog, silent and suffering. And the constant endeavor of the soul to rise and dominate, assert its independence, its equality, its right as good as anyone else's to its own peculiar way of living and thinking. No man is his brother's keeper. But for the poor the whole world is a self-constituted critic; your smallest action is open to debate. No secret place of your soul is safe from invasion. To have lived through it is rich experience, filling one's life with understanding and sympathy, helping one to be useful.

Everywhere and always I was conscious of the inevitable mystery of God's plan working through my life. It was as if I were but a vessel which God used in order to work out a certain purpose. Slowly the beneficence of suffering dawned upon me. A feeling came that we are here for growth and development, a thing not accomplished by ease and indolence.

With eyes then opened to a new vision, I walked the way of life. Sorrow was no longer hardship. Sickness and trouble were no longer hindrances. It was by these measures that a loving Providence was leading me to a broader outlook, a braver way of life. My duty and soon my pleasure was to accept the conditions and build upon them the edifice of life. Futile questions were stilled. Inequalities ceased to trouble. There was something in life higher than physical comfort and well-being; their opposites were fitting means for the work I had in hand. I began to understand a little of Christ's atonement. I too, was beginning to have a little of His at-one-ment. Life became rich in opportunity.

At one time I felt all the agony of the violin string when the master stretches and stretches it, tuning it to the proper pitch. Now that tuning has been accomplished for me and divine harmonies vibrate through my awaiting soul. Once I had felt like the wretched horses I had seen tugging helplessly at heavy loads or on the deadly treadmill, climbing an endless hill, monotonously dull, with limbs and back aching, no respite or goal in sight. But now life is a fairway or a race course for me, and I can pursue with swift and free decision the path toward my longed-for goal.

Apart from the philosophy I learned through bitter experience, certain inborn traits helped me. I have no sense of the value of money. It means nothing to me in itself. My brain does not register in terms of dollars and cents. And strangely enough, I have always felt this to be my greatest asset. You see it freed me from fear and released me from those small pitiful debates of the careful and particular. I worked very hard. I spent freely after figuring carefully and assuring myself of the accuracy of my figures, and then I sat back and waited for the results I had discounted. It was a gambler's method, but, controlled by the inexorable knowledge of two-plus-two, it carried me to success.

And then, being thoroughly illogical, I never allowed business to interfere with pleasure. For I have always enjoyed life in its every aspect. Anything from a peanut at the circus to a box at the opera may be sheer, unadulterated joy. In my hardest years, if an opportunity offered of a ride into the country with a friend or an afternoon under the soul-reviving influence of a symphony, I departed thereto. True, I worked half the night to make up, but you see by this time I had learned a little of how to use my body to liberate my spirit. Anyway, a few hours with Beethoven are more restful than sleep.

Riches and poverty do not lie in the acquisition of money or the lack of it. Money has very little to do with the riches of the soul, which in the end are all one has. There is even a certain impoverishment that comes with a motor and an apartment on a fashionable street. No, I don't mean their up-keep. I mean the humiliation, the poverty, that you are you, the same woman rich that you were poor, full of faults and a few virtues, making the same dull, inexcusable mistakes, but certainly striving always to improve. You the rich are no whit more attractive or capable than you who were poor and struggling a few years back. But when before you plodded lonely and unappreciated, now the glamour of the motor and the smart apartment surrounds you with a tangible glory. It is amazing how many friends look you up, call you by name, and extol you, who were once a little timid, or indifferent, or utterly neglectful in your time of dire poverty. One has true friends when one is poor and no riches can be greater than that. They are not so obvious when one is rich.

And the deep experience of the lonely climb on the mountain of success brings a wealth beyond power to compute. To you all suffering is under-standable and your heart opens wide in sympathy. To you illness is negligible. You have learned that you can dominate yourself. You know that your body lags, but your soul proceeds upon its triumphant way.

You realize the futility of worry. You learn to hate the small and the little. Life is a pie which you cut in large slices, not grudgingly, not sparingly. You know your limitations and proceed to eliminate them; your abilities, and proceed to develop them.

You are free. The small perplexities of small minds eddy and boil about you. Confident from the experience that has led you out of these same dangers, you attack each problem as it appears, unafraid. And a new philosophy is born, reversing all accepted creeds and rules. For you the precipitate of sorrow is happiness, the precipitate of struggle is success. Life means opportunity, and the thing men call death is the last wonderful, beautiful adventure.

> I go to prove my soul!
> I see my way as birds their trackless way.
> I shall arrive! what time, what circuit first,
> I ask not; but unless God send His hail
> Or blinding fireballs, sleet or stifling snow,
> In some time, His good time, I shall arrive:
> He guides me and the bird. In His good time!

CPSIA information can be obtained
at www.ICGtesting.com
Printed in the USA
BVOW09s0442121117

500069BV00007B/129/P